Passport's Illustrated Travel Guide to

GREECE

FROM
THOMAS
COOK

PASSPORT BOOKS
a division of *NTC Publishing Group*
Lincolnwood, Illinois USA

Published by Passport Books,
a division of NTC Publishing Group,
4255 W. Touhy Avenue,
Lincolnwood (Chicago), Illinois
60646–1975 U.S.A.

Written by Robin Gauldie

Original photography by Terry Harris

Edited, designed and produced by AA Publishing.
© The Automobile Association 1995.
Maps © The Automobile Association 1995.

Library of Congress Catalog Card Number: 94-68187

ISBN 0-8442-9073-4

The contents of this publication are believed correct at the time of
printing. Nevertheless, the publishers cannot accept responsibility for
any errors or omissions, or for changes in the details given in this guide
or for the consequences of any reliance on the information provided by
the same. Assessments of attractions, hotels, restaurants and so forth are
based upon the author's own experience and therefore descriptions given
in this guide necessarily contain an element of subjective opinion which
may not reflect the publisher's opinion or dictate a reader's own
experiences on another occasion.
**We have tried to ensure accuracy in this guide, but things do
change and we would be grateful if readers would advise us of any
inaccuracies they may encounter.**

Published by Passport Books in conjunction with AA Publishing and the
Thomas Cook Group Ltd.

Color separation: BTB Colour Reproduction, Whitchurch, Hampshire,
England.

Printed by: Edicoes ASA, Oporto, Portugal.

Contents

About this Book

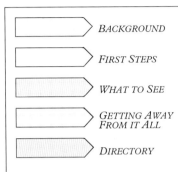

> BACKGROUND

> FIRST STEPS

> WHAT TO SEE

> GETTING AWAY FROM IT ALL

> DIRECTORY

This book is divided into five sections, identified by the above colour coding.

The **Background** gives an introduction to Greece – its history, geography, politics and culture.
First Steps offers practical advice on getting to grips with the language and customs of the country and getting around.

What to See is an alphabetical listing of places to visit, interspersed with walks and tours.
Getting Away From it All highlights places off the beaten track where it is possible to relax and enjoy peace and quiet.
Finally, the **Directory** provides practical information – from shopping and entertainment to children and sport, including a section on business matters. Special highly illustrated **features** on specific aspects of Greece appear throughout the book.

Mapping

The maps in this book use internationally recognised country abbreviations:
AL Albania BG Bulgaria TR Turkey

Donkeys and mules still play an important part in the life of many rural communities

BACKGROUND

> *Other countries may offer you discoveries*
> *in manners or lore or landscape; Greece offers you*
> *something harder – the discovery of yourself.*
> LAWRENCE DURRELL
> *Prospero's Cell* (1937)

Introduction

Greece is where the distant past and the vital present meet; a land of big cities and empty hillsides, snow-capped peaks and sandy beaches, ancient temples and busy summer holiday resorts. No other European country has such deep cultural roots, tapping into more than 4,000 years of Hellenic history – and few other European countries offer such a variety of things to do and places to see.

Apart from its ancient archaeological sites, mainland Greece offers some of the last wilderness areas and uncrowded beaches in Europe, many of them unknown to the millions who visit the Greek islands each year.

Though most Greeks have abandoned their colourful traditional costumes, the country's folklore still comes to life during the many summer festivals and saints' days, when Greeks celebrate with feasting, music and dancing.

Life is lived outdoors most of the year, and there is nothing to beat sitting

LOCATOR

Fishing boats at Astakos

MAINLAND GREECE

at a shady harbour-side table eating fish or octopus caught only that morning, with a glass of ice-cold beer or a carafe of strong-tasting *retsina*. Food in Greece is simple, hearty – and cheap.

In addition to the fine beaches, Greece offers ancient cities, lost temples, crusader castles and mighty sea fortresses amid striking scenery. For accommodation you can choose from bright, modern apartments and small hotels, big, bustling resorts, or comfortably restored traditional

mansions, castles or former monasteries.

Lovers of nature will find isolated mountain wildernesses and giant freshwater lakes which attract Europe's rarest birds, and fields and forests full of wild flowers and dazzling butterflies.

For those in search of sport, Greece offers the best yachting and windsurfing in Europe, plus waterskiing from dozens of sunny beaches, parascending, diving and snorkelling. Few other countries pack such an array of delights into such a small space.

History

BC

1700–1600
Mycenaean culture emerges on mainland.

1200
Collapse of Mycenaean culture.

1100
Arrival of the Dorian Greeks.

776
First Olympic Games.

800–600
City-state system takes shape.

490
First Persian invasion. Athenian victory at the battle of Marathon.

480
Second Persian invasion. Greek army annihilated at Thermopylae, and Athens captured. Persian navy defeated at Salamis.

479
Persians defeated at Plataiai and Mycale. End of the Persian Wars.

478
Athens at the height of its power as leader of the Delian League.

431–404
Peloponnesian War between Sparta and Athens ending in Athenian defeat.

371
Thebes defeats Sparta at the Battle of Lévktra.

359–336
Rise of Macedonia.

338
Macedonia defeats southern cities at Battle of Khairónia.

336–323
Reign of Alexander the Great.

The 'Mask of Agamemnon'

323–196
Macedonian kings.

200–146
Wars with Rome, culminating in the end of Greek and Macedonian independence.

AD

242–251
Goths appear on the Greek frontier for the first time.

260–268
Gothic raids into Greece begin.

324
The Roman Emperor Constantine moves his capital to Byzantium (Istanbul), renaming it Constantinople and founding the Christian (Byzantine) empire in Greece and the east.

393
Olympic Games banned by the Roman Emperor Theodosius.

529
Last schools of philosophy suppressed in Athens.

600–700
Pagan Slavs and Goths invade Greece as far as the Peloponnese.

800–900
Byzantine recovery.

1204
Frankish/Venetian Fourth Crusade sacks Constantinople. Franks and Venetians divide Greece.

1261–62
Byzantine Empire recovers Constantinople and most of mainland Greece.

1354
Ottoman Turks capture Gallipoli.

1429
Turks take Thessaloníki.
1453
Fall of Constantinople and the end of the Byzantine Empire.
1460
Fall of Mistra.
1499
Turks take Návpaktos, Koróni and Methóni from Venice.
1537–40
Turks take Monemvasía and Návplion.
1571
Turks checked at Battle of Lepanto by Holy League led by Don John of Austria.
1685–99
Venice recovers the Peloponnese.
1821–30
War of Independence. The Peloponnese, Athens and Attica, Sterea Ellas, the Cyclades and the Argo-Saronic islands become the new Republic of Greece.
1831
President Capodistrias assassinated.
1833
Bavarian Prince Otto becomes King Otho I of the Hellenes.
1881
Turkey cedes Thessaly to Greece.
1912
First Balkan War. Greece gains Thessaloniki, Ionina and Epirus from Turkey.
1913
Second Balkan War. Greece allied with Serbia against Bulgaria.
1917
Greece joins World War I on the side of Britain and France.
1919
Encouraged by Britain and France, Greece lands troops at Smyrna (Izmir) in Turkey.
1920–23
War between Greece and Turkey ends in

defeat for Greece. Around one million Greeks driven from Turkey; 400,000 Muslims driven out of Greece.
1924–36
Political chaos, leading to suspension of constitution. General Metaxas becomes dictator.
1939
Italy invades Albania.
1940
Italy demands access to Greek ports. Metaxas refuses. Italian invasion defeated in Epirus.
1941–1944
German occupation. Varied resistance groups active in many areas, including growing Communist faction.
1946–49
Civil war, with the USA and Britain supporting the Royalist right-wing government forces against the Communists.
1967–74
Military junta rules Greece, led by Colonel Papadopoulos. King Constantine expelled. Referendum ends the monarchy.
1974
Collapse of the junta after the Turkish invasion of Cyprus. Restoration of democracy.
1981
Greece joins the European Community. Left-wing PASOK party led by Andreas Papandreou elected.
1984
PASOK re-elected.
1989
PASOK defeated. Series of short-lived caretaker governments.
1990
Nea Dimokratia party elected under Konstantinos Mitsotakis.
1993
PASOK re-elected.

Empires, Hegemonies and Invasions

The Mycenaeans and Dorians

These Bronze Age warriors built citadels ringed by massive boulder walls in the Peloponnese, Athens, Thebes and elsewhere, and traded with Egypt and the empires of the Middle East. Their civilisation toppled around 1200BC. About 150 years later, the first Greek-speaking, iron-using Dorians arrived from the north, settled among the ruins of the Mycenaean civilisation, and over the next 300 years developed their own culture.

Silver head of a bull (*rhyton*) found at Mycenae, dating from the 16th century BC

The city-states

By the 8th century BC Greece was divided among dozens of small, fiercely independent city-states. Not all were Athenian-style democracies. Sparta was an authoritarian, militarised state ruled by two kings. Other cities were democracies, oligarchies controlled by a group of powerful men, or tyrannies under an absolute ruler. The rival cities banded together against Persia in the early 5th century BC, but after the invasion Athens and Sparta fought each other for almost 30 years. Sparta, the victor in 404BC, was in turn defeated by Thebes, which dominated Greece until the rise of Macedonia (see page 132).

The Macedonians and Hellenistic Greece

Macedonia and a number of smaller kingdoms created by Alexander's generals dominated the Greek world from the end of the 4th century BC until the Roman conquest. Other Hellenistic kingdoms were created in the Middle East, giving the Greeks broader horizons. Despite political chaos and frequent conflict among Alexander's successors, trade, philosophy and the arts flourished in the wider Greek world, but the mainland cities stagnated.

The Romans in Greece

Roman legions first landed in Greece in 201BC. Over the next century Rome became increasingly powerful and was frequently at war with Macedonia. Greek cities which resisted Roman hegemony were destroyed, as Corinth was in 146BC. The Roman conquest was completed in 86BC when Athens fell, bringing almost three centuries of stability, during which Athens flourished with the building of a new Roman city beside the ancient Greek one. Corinth, too, was rebuilt and in the later Roman period Thessaloníki became a great trade centre.

The Byzantine Empire

In AD330 the Roman Emperor Constantine dedicated his new capital of Byzantium (now Istanbul) and renamed it Constantinople. The city became the heart of a Christian empire which was more Greek than Roman, with territory which included all of Greece and Asia Minor and much of the Middle East. It lasted for more than 1,000 years, withstanding invasions by Slavs, Bulgars, Persians, Saracens and Turks until its final defeat in 1453.

The Venetians

Venice, with its eyes on the Greek islands, encouraged its Frankish allies of the Fourth Crusade to sack Constantinople in 1204. The Venetians then seized Évvoia (Evia), the Ionian islands, and strategic harbours throughout Greece. When Constantinople fell to the Turks, the Venetians held on to mainland and island strongholds including Monemvasía, Methóni and Koróni,

Top: bronze helmet of Miltiades, hero of the battle of Marathón, found at Olympia (490BC)
Left: bronze head of a 5th-century BC Athenian warrior

Návplion, Návpaktos, Rion and Andírrion, and as late as the end of the 17th century reconquered most of the Peloponnese from Turkey before being finally driven out of the mainland for good in 1715.

The Turks in Greece

The Turkish conquest cut Greece off from the Christian West but made it part of a vast Muslim Ottoman empire. The seafaring Greeks carried on much of the trade of this empire, and Greek traders and shipbuilders flourished. The Turks tolerated other religions but punished rebellion with extreme ferocity. Despite this, risings against the Turks were frequent. In 1821 a final struggle for independence began, leading to the creation of the first independent Greek state in 1830.

Politics

*P*olitics is a favourite topic of Greek conversation. Memories of the 1946–9 Civil War and of the 1967–74 military junta have begun to fade, but political discussion is guaranteed to raise voices and tempers and the fiercest debate is often between those who are on the same side. In 1993 passionate protest followed the unofficial visit of ex-king Constantine, who had been rejected in the referendum of 1973.

Since 1974, Greece has been a parliamentary democracy with an elected president whose role is mainly ceremonial. Real power is in the hands of an elected prime minister.

Political parties

Two major parties dominate Greek politics. PASOK, a left-wing alliance, ruled through much of the 1980s, was voted out in 1989 and returned to power in 1993. The aggressively right-wing Nea Dimokratia (New Democracy) party, in power between 1990 and 1993, made itself unpopular by a wide-ranging programme of privatisation of state enterprises and a drive to collect tax from a workforce which is nearly 50 per cent self-employed.

Nea Dimokratia was toppled by the defection of one of its ministers, Antonios Samaras, whose Politiki Anoikti (Political Spring) party campaigned on a fiercely nationalist platform to win a handful of seats.

Two other minority parties, the old-style KKE (Greek Communist Party) and a reformed socialist party, are also represented in the national parliament.

Left: Vouli (parliament building) in Athens
Bottom: PASOK's leader, Andreas Papandreou

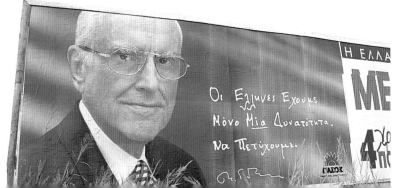

Campaign posters flash all the colours of the Greek political spectrum

Greece and Europe

Anything touching on Greece's hard-won sovereignty quickly becomes a hot political issue, often overshadowing rational discussion of the shaky state of the Greek economy – partly kept afloat by the European Union – which has urged Greece to privatise its unwieldy nationalised enterprises and reduce a huge economic deficit. Modernisation measures (including higher taxes) are widely disliked and universally blamed on Brussels, but many Greeks seem able to ignore the visible benefits of EU membership.

The PASOK government, which was stridently anti-American during its first two terms, began its third spell in office with peace overtures towards the USA, partly to balance grass-roots anti-European feeling.

Neighbouring Turkey, though a NATO ally, is still seen as a threat, and Greece spends proportionately more on defence than any other European country. The hottest issue in recent years has been Macedonia – a name to which Greece claims sole rights but which is also claimed by the former Yugoslav republic across the border. Greek ministers refuse to recognise the newly independent state under that name, referring to it instead as the Republic of Skopje (after its capital) or as FYROM, an acronym for Former Yugoslav Republic of Macedonia. Recognition of the former Yugoslav republic by European nations brought howls of protest from Greece.

THE COLONELS' JUNTA

On 21 April 1967 a group of army officers staged a *coup d'état* to prevent the election of a left-wing government. The junta, led by Colonel Yioryios Papadopoulos, censored the press, banned trade unions, imprisoned thousands of opponents and banned free speech, popular music, short skirts, long hair and beards. Despite this mixture of terror and petty stupidity, the colonels were strongly supported by the USA, and many Greeks believe their *coup* was a CIA plot. The junta fell in 1974 after its backing for a right-wing Greek coup in Cyprus led to Turkish invasion of the island.

POLITICS AND PHILOSOPHY

...Plato points upward to heaven, Aristotle downward to the earth.
Clement C J Webb, *A History of Philosophy*, Oxford University Press (1915)

Athens was the most democratic of the Greek city-states, but it was a strictly limited democracy. Only free men born in the city might vote, and even at the best of times the man in the street might be more easily inspired by charismatic orators than by level-headed statesmen.

Philosophical debate was as intense as political argument, and the philosophers who entered political discussion are those best known today.

The philosophers who took an active part in the political life of the city are nevertheless outnumbered by those who stood aloof from it, preferring the discussion of ideals to realities. In fact, the schools of Hellenic philosophy flowered in the 4th and 3rd centuries BC, when Athens was no longer the greatest power in the Greek world, and many of the most influential teachers argued for individual self-sufficiency rather than engagement with the fickle world. To the Ancient Greeks, 'philosopher' meant no more than 'lover of knowledge', and philosophy embraced the entire realm of thought from pure mathematics to morality and ethics.

and arguably the most influential on later Western thinkers. Much of his rigorously logical thinking aimed to explain organic and physical phenomena; today, he might be a physicist rather than a philosopher.

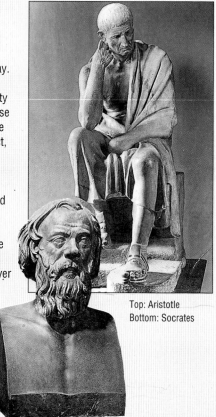

Top: Aristotle
Bottom: Socrates

ARISTOTLE (843–322BC)

The tutor of Alexander the Great and pupil of Plato (his name means 'the best student'), he is the least mystical of the Greeks

IN ANCIENT ATHENS

DEMOCRITUS (c.460–c.370BC)

A contemporary of Plato, Democritus argued that the world could not be perceived through the senses alone but must be understood intellectually. He conceived the universe as consisting of tiny, indestructible units, for which he coined the term 'atoms'.

DIOGENES OF SINOPE (c. 410–c.320BC)

Founder of the school of philosophers called the Cynics, Diogenes might be called the first drop-out. He argued for the simple life and rejected the everyday demands of convention, owned as little as possible and lived in a barrel.

The death of Socrates, by Jacques-Louis David (19th century)

EPICURUS (341–270BC)

Epicurus and his followers argued that there is no after-life and that therefore happiness in this one is the chief good, and therefore the only reasonable aim.

PLATO (427–347BC)

Plato is among the best-known of all the Greek philosophers, not only because he was the most prolific writer but because so many of his writings have survived. His central argument was that deeper nature and the meaning of things could be determined only by thought, not through the senses.

SOCRATES (469–399BC)

Socrates lived and taught when Athens was at its zenith, paving the way for all those who came after him. He left no writings of his own, but is known to us through the work of his followers Plato and Xenophon, and his opponent the playwright Aristophanes, who caricatured him in his play The Clouds. His championing of reason over superstition and his delight in argument for its own sake made him many enemies among Athenian conservatives, who ultimately succeeded in having him tried and convicted on a charge of corrupting Athenian youth. The penalty was death by poison. Socrates might have escaped execution by pleading guilty, but refused to do so.

ZENO OF CITIUM (334–262BC)

Zeno and his followers, the Stoics (who take their name from the stoa or porch of the market-place where they gathered), held that the world was ordered by a divine reason, and Stoic influences are apparent in Christianity. Both Stoics and Cynics were more concerned with finding a philosophy suited to everyday life than with ultimate truths, and the debate which they started continues, one way or another, today.

Culture

New ways for old

Visitors to Greece only a quarter of a century ago might have seen grain being threshed on a stone threshing-floor, taken to the mill by mules, ground by wind-power and baked in a wood-fired village oven.

Pack-mules still carry heavy loads in villages all over Greece

Greece has come a long way since then. Mules are still useful load-carriers all over the country, but they are no longer the lifeline of many villages. New roads and shiny pick-up trucks are the signs of a new prosperity.

Windows on the world

Television, no longer an unattainable luxury, is a fixture in most Greek homes. Video and satellite TV have turned out-of-the-way hamlets into suburbs of the global information village. Taverna-owners who used to add up the bill on the paper tablecloth or the back of a cigarette packet are now just as likely to use a brand-new personal computer, and although it can take up to two years to have a telephone installed, many shepherds and villagers find cheap

walkie-talkies a convenient substitute. Fishermen, too, benefit from new technology, and most of the larger vessels have ship-to-shore radio and radar.

The tourism boom

Transport within Greece has become faster and more efficient. Perhaps even more importantly, for a country cut off by sea and international politics from its Western European trading partners, international transport links have improved. Holiday jets bring millions of tourists into Athens and other mainland airports at Kalamata, Préveza and Thessaloníki, but they also take Greeks abroad.

Change for the better?

Not all the changes have been positive – at least from the visitor's point of view. Those seeking tranquillity will be disappointed by the national fondness for massively amplified music and unsilenced motorcycles, and the microwave oven has done more to undermine the reputation of Greek cooking than oil or garlic ever

New prosperity buys bigger bikes

could. Traffic in Athens has grown worse with more widespread car ownership. Having said that, however, Greece is still a wonderful place in which to get away from it all, and much of the country away from the main tourist resorts remains completely unspoilt.

The Greeks abroad

During the 19th century millions of Greeks emigrated. There are large Greek communities in the USA, Canada, Australia and South Africa, all of them aiming to strike it rich and return home. Visitors who have seen hard-working expatriate Greeks in action may be surprised by how laid-back they seem to be in Greece.

A brighter future for Greece has also encouraged many younger overseas Greeks to return, often bringing fresh ideas and initiatives to the conservative villages their grandparents left. Many young men are put off by the prospect of a spell in uniform. All Greek men must spend two years in the armed forces on turning 21, and these reluctant soldiers are paid only a pittance.

Other Greeks have returned to the land of their ancestors after an even longer absence. As early as the 4th century BC, Greeks had settled on the shores of the Black Sea. With the fall of the Byzantine Empire, they preferred the rule of a Russian Orthodox tsar to that of an Ottoman Muslim sultan. Until the collapse of the USSR, 400,000 Greeks lived in the Soviet republics, many of whom have now chosen to live in Greece.

Greek personality

You may well meet an Aristotle (Aristotelis) in the corner store or find that your waiter's name is Socrates, but modern Greeks seem to have surprisingly

THOMAS COOK'S
Greece

Thomas Cook first visited Greece as part of a tour to the Nile, Palestine, Turkey and Italy in 1869; the party visited Epirus to see the ruins. By 1870 Athens was included in many of Cook's tours to Italy and Switzerland and an office was opened in Athens in Place Royale (now Platia Syntagma) in 1883. The building of Greek railways and interest aroused by archaeological excavations ensured a constant stream of customers for Cook's Greek tours. The restarting of the original Olympic Games in Athens in 1896 also attracted many visitors. The first conducted tour to Greece took place in 1904.

The company of contemporaries

little in common with their heroic ancestors. There is still a real pride in their achievements, and today's Greeks have inherited the philosopher's delight in ideas and debate, but 2,500 years of change separate them from the builders of the Parthenon. On first acquaintance, Greeks may seem indifferent one moment and pushy the next, but they become firm friends more quickly than any people in Europe.

Geography

Mainland Greece covers some 130,000 sq km. To the west, the Adriatic separates it from Italy. To the south lies the Mediterranean and to the east are the Aegean and its islands. Greece has some of the most spectacular landscapes and wide open spaces in Europe, from the peaks of Ólimbos (Olympus) to the rolling farmlands of Thrace.

Much of the country is mountainous, and throughout history the mountains have provided a defence against invasion and a refuge for those resisting occupying powers. Wherever you are in Greece there are mountains on the horizon, and you are never more than a few hours' drive from the sea.

Economy and population

Greece has a population of 10.5 million, more than 4 million of whom live in and around Athens. More than one in three Greeks work on the land, many of them on small, family-owned farms, and almost half are self-employed. It is still a poor country, and many people hold down several jobs in order to make ends meet. Money sent home by Greeks living overseas helps many families manage.

Farming

Oranges and lemons, cotton, tobacco, grapes and, above all, olives grow in abundance in the fertile valleys and plains and are among the country's major exports. Sheep and goats graze on higher, barren ground.

Flora and fauna

Intense farming has taken its toll of Greek wildlife over thousands of years, as it has throughout Europe, but low population density has left niches for many rare and endangered species (see pages 138–9).

Geology and climate

Beneath the thin topsoil, most of Greece is porous limestone. Water drains through it quickly, giving mountains and hillsides a parched, near-desert look for much of the year. Underground rivers have cut through the rock in many places, creating echoing caverns lined with coloured spires and stalactites. Topsoil washed from the mountainsides has accumulated over millennia in fertile valleys watered by rivers which swell with winter rains and melting snow but

A prickly pear cactus clings to the barren rocks of the *kastro* at Monemvasía

The northern Pindhos mountain range is one of the last areas of wilderness in southern Europe

dwindle to a trickle in the hot summers. Winters are short, mild and wet on the plains and around the coasts, but can be bitterly cold in the mountains.

The sea

If the mountains defend and divide Greece, the sea unites it with the outside world and provides a living for thousands of sailors and fishermen. The Greek merchant navy is one of the world's biggest and rivals tourism as the country's biggest foreign currency earner and one of its biggest employers. All over Greece you will meet retired seamen whose encyclopaedic knowledge of the world's ports comes from a spell on one of the thousands of tankers and freighters which fly the blue and white colours of Greece. Ready access to the sea also made it easy for Greeks to leave their country when times were hard, and more than 4 million Greeks live overseas, most of them in the USA, Australia, Canada and South Africa – though it is said that you can find a Greek in any seaport in the world.

In ancient times the sea linked the enterprising Greeks with the great empires of the Middle East, and adventurous mariners from the Greek city-states founded colonies as far afield as Marseilles and Sicily in the west and the shores of the Black Sea in the east. Well into this century it was easier to travel by sea than by road and little mainland ports like Yíthion, Neapoli or Yerolimín were thriving centres of import and export to Athens and abroad. Much of their trade now goes by road, and these sleepy, forgotten harbours with their rows of merchants' mansions are some of the pleasantest places in which to spend a Greek holiday.

ENVIRONMENT

Greece's record on the environment could be better. There are no votes in cleaning up rivers, seas and countryside at the expense of farmers, fishermen or industrialists, so Greek governments tend to ignore environmental issues. Interference (or even comment) from abroad is widely resented, and Greeks often argue that the tourists who complain about litter-strewn beaches are the very people who create the litter. They have a point, but the heaps of festering garbage which accumulate wherever there is space to pull off the road are not the work of visitors. Unfortunately, local authorities have neither the money nor the powers to clean up the mess, and national government in Athens has yet to show any real interest in doing so.

Less obvious to the holiday visitor is the environmental damage being inadvertently caused by misdirected European Union investment. Greece, the poorest country in the EU, is a major beneficiary of its regional funds, and Greek farmers have been quick to see the benefits of the EU's agricultural subsidy system. On the mainland, tobacco and cotton cultivation is booming as never before and European glut of both crops means farmers are paid to plough them back into the soil. The farmers can hardly be blamed for trying to make easy money, but the consequences are worrying. Many of Greece's rivers have been reduced to a mere trickle by dams built to meet the country's fast-growing need for hydroelectric power. At their mouths, delta wetlands which shelter thousands of rare birds are being drained by tobacco and cotton farmers. Greece's longest and mightiest river, the Akhelóös (see pages 94–5), is threatened by a new set of dams which will cut off water from the wetlands at its mouth, drown a remote and historic monastery and village in the Píndhos mountains, and cut off water from existing dams down river. Ironically, the EU, which is backing the multi-million ECU project, has already prosecuted Greece in the European Court for failing to protect the same wetlands that the dam threatens.

Huge man-made lakes, like this one near Marathón, have changed Greece's landscape

FIRST STEPS

You know what the Greeks are like; we can't talk without using our hands.
BUS DRIVER
quoted by Patrick Leigh Fermor in
Roumeli: Travels in Northern Greece (1966)

THE ALPHABET AND VOCABULARY

Romanised spellings of Greek names can vary. In placename headings and in the index, this book uses the transliterations which correspond to AA maps. More familiar Anglicised spellings (given in brackets in the headings) are sometimes used in the text. This leads to inconsistencies when compared with other books and maps: *Nafplion, Navplion, Nauplion, Nafplio, Navplio* and *Nauplio* are all the same town. The differences are rarely so great as to make a name unrecognisable. The names of museums and other places of interest may also be translated differently, so that what one source interprets as 'Historical and Ethnological Museum' may be translated elsewhere as 'National Historical Museum'. To avoid confusion, placename headings give the name in romanised Greek, followed by the most usual English translation in brackets.

It is helpful to know the Greek alphabet so that you can recognise placenames, while the few words and phrases following the alphabet will also come in handy.

Alphabet

Alpha	short *a*, as in hat	Iota	short *i* sound, as in hit	Sigma	*s* sound
Beta	*v* sound			Taf	*t* sound
Gamma	*y* sound, as in you	Kappa	*k* sound	Ipsilon	long *e*, as in feet
Delta	*th* sound, as in father	Lambda	*l* sound		
		Mu	*m* sound	Phi	*f* sound
Epsilon	short *e*	Nu	*n* sound	Chi	guttural *ch* sound, as in lock
Zita	*z* sound	Omicron	*o*		
Eta	long *e*, as in feet	Pi	*p* sound		
Theta	hard *th* sound, as in think	Rho	*r* sound	Psi	*ps*, as in lamps
				Omega	*o*

Basic vocabulary

good morning	*kalimera*
good evening	*kalispera*
goodnight	*kalinikhta*
hello	*yasou*
thank you	*efkharisto*
please/you're welcome	*parakalo*
yes	*ne*
no	*ochi*
where is...?	*pou ine?*
how much is...?	*poso kani?*
do you speak English?	*milate anglika?*
I don't speak Greek	*dhen milo ellinik*

Travelling

car	*avtokiniton*
bus	*leoforion*
ferry	*plion*
train	*trenon*
airport	*aerolimenon*
ticket	*isitirion*

Places

street	*odhos*
square	*platia*
avenue	*leoforos*
restaurant	*estiatorion*
hotel	*xenodochio*
room	*dhomatio*
post office	*tachidhromio*
police	*astinomia*
pharmacy	*farmakio*
doctor	*iatros*
bank	*trapeza*
café	*kafeneion*

Food and drink

food	*fagito*
bread	*psomi*
water	*nero*
wine	*krasi*
beer	*bira*
coffee	*kafes*
lobster	*astakos*
squid	*kalamares/kalama rakia*
otopus	*oktapodhi*
red mullet	*barbounia*
whitebait	*maridhes*
lamb	*arni*
chicken	*kotopoulo*
meat balls	*keftedhes*
skewered meat	*souvlakia*
pork	*chirini*
spinach	*spanaki*
courgette	*kolokithia*
beans	*fasoles*
chips	*patates tiganites*
cucumber	*angouri*
tomato	*tomata*
olives	*elies*
salad with feta	*horiatiki*
tomato salad	*salata*
yoghurt and cucumber dip	*tsatsiki*

PLACENAMES

Where a widely used English version of a placename exists, this is used throughout the text except in the initial placename heading. Such placenames include:

Athens (*Athínai*)
Corinth (*Kórinthos*)
Delphi (*Delfí*)
Epirus (*Ípiros*)
Kalamata (*Kalámai*)
Macedonia (*Makedhonía*)
Patras (*Pátrai*)
Sparta (*Spárti*)
Thebes (*Thívai*)
Thessaly (*Thessalía*)
Thrace (*Thráki*)

Postal addresses and street names

Odhos (street), *platia* (place or square) and *leoforos* (avenue) are usually dropped from Greek postal addresses. In this book, *odhos* and *leoforos* have accordingly been ommitted but, in the interests of clarity, *platia* (as in Platia Sindagma) has been retained.

Numbers

1	*ena*	14	*dhekatessera*
2	*dhio*	15	*dhekapende*
3	*tria*	16	*dhekaexi*
4	*tessera*	17	*dhekaevta*
5	*pende*	18	*dhekaokto*
6	*exi*	19	*dhekenea*
7	*evta*	20	*ikosi*
8	*okhto*	30	*trianda*
9	*enea*	40	*seranda*
10	*dheka*	50	*peninda*
11	*endheka*	100	*ekaton*
12	*dhodheka*	1000	*khilies*
13	*dhekatria*		

LANGUAGE, MANNERS AND CUSTOMS

Hospitality

Greek hospitality is legendary. Traditionally, any stranger is a guest. That attitude of *philoxenia* ('love of guests') is dying hard with the growth of tourism, but it quickly starts to show itself as you travel away from the busy resorts – or even in them at less busy times of the year. A gift of a flower from someone's garden, nuts or fruit from an orchard you pass, or a carafe of wine sent to your table by a complete stranger comes as a surprise to visitors from less warm-hearted lands. It should come as no surprise, though, in a land where the trading tradition goes back 3,000 years, that Greeks can also drive a hard bargain.

Queuing

Queuing for public transport is virtually unheard of, and you must expect a certain amount of pushing and shoving on boarding boats, trains and urban buses. In banks and post offices, however, there is usually a fairly orderly queue – though if you do not step forward promptly when it is your turn, somebody else will.

Dress code

Topless sunbathing is now accepted on even the most public beaches, but total nudity will offend and may get you arrested. Shorts and T-shirts are acceptable summer wear everywhere except on visits to monasteries and churches, where men must wear long trousers, women skirts which cover the knees, and both sexes should wear long sleeves.

Women travellers

Greece is still a male-dominated society (though it is changing) but many women feel less risk of harassment than in many other Mediterranean countries. Greek men certainly feel that a woman can only be flattered by their attention, but are unlikely to persist in the face of an unambiguous 'no'. You are more likely to meet with unwanted attention in summer resorts – from summer visitors – than from local people elsewhere.

Language

The Greek language can be intimidating, if only because its alphabet is so different from the familiar Roman script, but a little Greek goes a very long way in making friends and influencing people.

Older Greeks like this retired shepherd jealously guard the tradition of *philoxenia*

A local farmer and his mule enjoy the contentment that a slower pace of life generates

Greeks firmly believe that their language is almost impossible for foreigners to learn, and even knowledge of a few simple phrases will be admired and extravagantly praised.

Greeks use a lot of body language (they say that to silence a Greek you need only tie his hands behind his back) which can be helpful and confusing by turns. One helpful hint: a backward jerk of the head which you might interpret as a nod is exactly the opposite. Often accompanied by a click of the tongue, it means 'no'. On the other hand, a rapid side-to-side shake of the head is not a negative – it means anything from 'I don't understand' to 'What can I do for you?'

The Greek alphabet is impossible to translate directly into other languages, and vice versa: it takes a while to puzzle out that *xampourgker* means 'hamburger' or *kroyasan* means 'croissant'. Some Roman letters are missing from the Greek alphabet, and are represented by combining two Greek letters to make the appropriate sound. *Mu* and *pi* are combined to make a hard B as in bar; *nu* and *taf* to make a hard D as in dog; and *nu* and *kappa* are often used to approximate a hard G as in golf.

The white pebble beach at Ayios Ioannis, on the east coast of the Pílion (Pelion) peninsula

WHERE TO GO

Mainland Greece has more than enough sights and landscapes to fill any holiday and offers endless scope for exploration off the beaten track.

Ancient Greece

The ruins of ancient cities and temples clutter any map of Greece, but surprisingly few of the ancient sites which are so carefully marked and signposted are of interest to anyone except the keen archaeologist. They are, after all, up to 4,000 years old, and time has taken its toll. Even the best-preserved or most lovingly restored buildings lack roofs and many of the columns which supported them, while the statues and friezes which decorated them are either in museums or have been carted off by looters. The less well-preserved sites may be marked only by a single column, a scattering of masonry blocks, and a few holes in the ground. Of the scores of ancient sites carefully marked by the Greek Ministry of Culture, those of central Athens (see pages 36–9) and a dozen or so others are guaranteed not to disappoint. These include the Temple of Poseidon at Soúnion (see pages 48 and 54–5); Mikínai (Mycenae); Árgos and Tiryns in the Argolid; the nearby Theatre of Epídhavros (see pages 62–3), and Corinth (see page 68); Olympia in the western Peloponnese (see page 78); and Delphi in the Sterea Ellas region (see pages 88–9). Equally impressive are the remains of the temple complex at Dhodhóni in Epirus (see page 104), and the sites of the lost cities of Dhion, below Mount Olympus (see page 128), and Philippi (see page 120). In the southern Peloponnese, the mighty walls of ancient Ithomi are worth a detour.

Battlefields

Those interested in military history may like to visit the well-signposted battlefields where the decisive conflicts of classical Greece were fought out. A crescent of battlefields lies north of Athens, with Marathón (see page 50) to the northeast, while Thermopylae (see page 53), Lévktra (see page 53), Plataiaí (see page 53) and Chaironeia (see page 86) lie to the northwest. All five are within easy reach of Athens.

Beaches

Mainland Greece offers excellent beaches, many of them surprisingly uncrowded. The longest and least developed sandy beaches run for many kilometres down the west coast of the Peloponnese, and in the southern Peloponnese there are also excellent sand beaches at Koróni, Methóni and Stoupa (see pages 64–5 and 76–7). The more sheltered east coast of the Peloponnese boasts many delightful little beaches of white pebbles and coarse shingle.

In the north, there are excellent sand beaches on the Khalkidhikí (Chalkidiki) peninsulas (see pages 122–3), at Párga (see page 107) on the west coast, and near Préveza (see page 107).

Castles
Lovers of medieval romance should head for the Peloponnese, where it seems as though every hilltop and mountain pass is crowned by a Byzantine, Frankish or Turkish castle and every harbour has its Venetian fortress. Among the most striking are those at Mistra and Yeráki (see pages 74–5), Monemvasía (see pages 72–3), Koróni, Methóni and Pílos (see pages 64–5) and Chlemoútsi (see pages 78–9).

Historic towns
Towns with historic quarters which have survived the ravages of war, fire, earthquake and modernisation are easiest to find in the northern mainland. They include Ioánnina (see page 104), Kastoría (see page 128), Kaválla, Komotiní and Xánthi (see pages 120–1). In the south, Návplion (see page 61) has a pretty town centre dating from its 18th-century Venetian heyday.

Mountains
The finest mountain scenery in Greece is to be found in the Pindhos range, which forms the backbone of the northern mainland. The Parnassós massif is an awesomely beautiful backdrop to Delphi, and the lonely peaks of Olympus dominate the plains of Thessaly and Macedonia. In the Peloponnese, the saw-edged ridge of the Taíyetos runs from the north to meet the sea at Ákra Taínaron (Cape Matapan), the southernmost tip of mainland Greece.

Picturesque villages
Mainland villages display a rich variety of traditional architectural styles, from the ruined towers of the Mani (see pages 70–1 and 80–1) to the half-timbered mansions of the Pílion (Pelion) peninsula (see pages 112–13), the stone-slab homes of the Zagória (see pages 114–15) or the mud-brick ghost villages around the Préspa lakes (see page 129).

The slopes of the Parnassós massif, backdrop for the beauties of ancient Delphi

DRIVING

Driving in Greece requires a combination of caution, confidence and strong nerves. Roads have been improved greatly in recent years and most are now well-surfaced but Greece is a mountainous country and there are many steep hairpin bends. Greek bus drivers, who like to take these hairpins at speed, usually sound their horns almost continuously to tell you that they are coming. Among other typically Greek hazards are flocks of goats or sheep being herded across the main road, usually when you least expect them.

In places, wide, newly tarred roads degenerate abruptly and without warning into pot-holed tracks, a spine-jarring experience for driver and passengers. Greek drivers will take an ordinary saloon car over the roughest roads, but off the beaten track some roads are suitable only for four-wheel-drive vehicles.

Outside the three major cities and the main highways which connect them traffic is light. In the cities, it is another story: driving, navigating and finding somewhere to park can be demanding, and it is easier to leave your car and explore on foot or by public transport. There are one-way systems in even the smallest villages. These are widely ignored by locals.

Greeks are aggressive drivers, and a combination of winding roads and cavalier driving habits results in the worst road accident level in Europe, with almost 2,000 fatalities a year. Speed limits are treated with contempt (Greek drivers flash their lights at oncoming traffic to warn of police checkpoints) and though seat belts are compulsory for drivers and front-seat passengers it is unlikely that you will ever see a Greek wearing one.

If all this sounds intimidating, do not let it deter you from driving in Greece. Driving can be by far the best way to see the country, and a car will take you to places impossible to reach by public transport. The golden rule for drivers in Greece is: expect the unexpected.

Toll booths on the major highways help return the cost of road construction

WHAT TO SEE

Aloof they crown the foreland lone
From aloft they loftier rise –
Fair columns, in the aureola rolled
From sunned Greek seas and skies.
HERMAN MELVILLE
Off Cape Colonna (1819–91)

Athínai

(Athens)

CENTRAL ATHENS

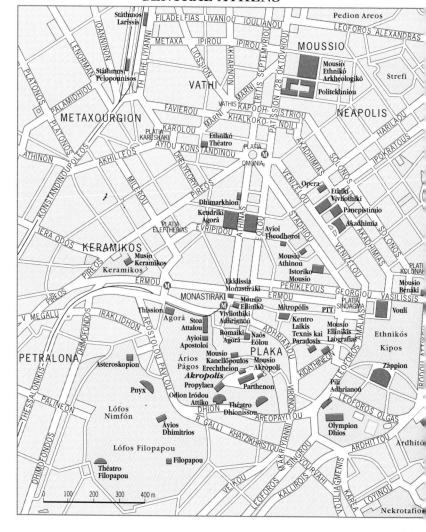

*A*thens is home to almost half the country's total population, and the glowing columns of the Parthenon, the city's best-loved landmark, rise above the crag of the Acropolis like an island of grace in a modern urban sea.

Much of Athens is surprisingly new, built since World War II to house an influx of people from the countryside. In 1940 only 850,000 people lived in the city. By 1970, there were 2.5 million. Today there are 4 million.

The city's apartment and office blocks nevertheless conceal happy surprises. Turn any corner and you may find yourself looking at a 1,000-year-old church, a tiny park cluttered with toppled ancient columns, a quaint old taverna or the high garden wall of a 19th-century mansion surrounded by exotic palm trees.

Athens has only one major city-centre park, Ethnikós Kípos (National Gardens), but makes up for its shortage of public green space with explosions of greenery and colour from gardens, balconies and window-boxes. Planes and orange trees line streets and squares, jasmine and honeysuckle cling to tumbledown walls and in spring even wasteland and roadside blaze briefly with wild poppies and daisies.

City life echoes the laid-back style of a rural village, and few corners are without a vendor peddling barbecued corn-cobs, nuts, sunflower seeds, or sesame-seed rings.

Most offices close for an afternoon siesta, and Athenians spend much leisure time playing backgammon or (as befits folk who live in the city where democracy was born) arguing politics at café tables.

Most of the city's ancient sites and museums are in a compact area within a 2-km radius of Platía Sindagma (Constitution Square), the hub of modern Athens.

Akropolis
(Acropolis)

*T*ime and weather have stripped the buildings of the Acropolis to bare white marble, making the perfect simplicity of their proportions all the more striking. Their impact reaches across more than two millennia.

The Temple of Athena Nike was restored in the 19th century

The 100m limestone crag was first occupied more than 5,000 years ago, and there are traces of Mycenaean buildings dating from 1500BC. In the 5th century BC Pericles – the city's leading statesman and its guiding hand from 461 to 430BC – commissioned Kallikrates and Iktinos (both after 450BC) to rebuild the temples sacked by the Persians in 480BC, and the brilliant Phidias (500–432BC) to design their friezes and statues.

Later occupiers demolished some buildings. Others (including the Parthenon) were damaged or destroyed during the many sieges of the Acropolis between medieval and modern times. As late as the War of Independence, Greek rebels used it as a fortress.

The main buildings of the site are linked by the Sacred Way, running from the middle gate of the Propylaia to the Parthenon. The site is entered by the eastern Beulé Gate, to the left of which stands the plinth of a statue to the Roman general Agrippa.
Acropolis (tel: 3210 219). Open: weekdays, 8am–4.45pm; weekends and holidays, 8.30am–2.45pm. Admission charge includes entry to museum and Acropolis site.

Erechtheion
Restored in the 1980s, the Erechtheion was the Acropolis's holiest shrine, dedicated to Athena as patroness of Athens. Standing opposite the Parthenon, its three Ionic porticos were built on different levels. The original *caryatids* (female figures) of the south portico have been replaced by copies.

Mousío Akropoli (Acropolis Museum)
Collection includes figures of Athena, 6th-century BC *korae* (figures of draped maidens), friezes from the Erechtheion and the Temple of Athena Nike, and *caryatids* from the Erechtheion.
Tel: 3236 665. Open: Monday, 11am–4.30pm; Tuesday to Friday, 8am–4.30pm; weekends, 8.30am–2.30pm.

Naos Athena Nike (Temple of Athena Nike)

The temple honours Athena as goddess of victory. Designed by Kallikrates in the mid-5th century BC to celebrate the Athenian defeat of Persia, it was completed in 424BC. Demolished by the Turks, it was restored in the 19th century.

Parthenon

Phidias and his patron Pericles intended the Parthenon to be an act of worship in stone, celebrating Athens at the zenith of its power.

Dedicated to Athena in 438BC, the Parthenon was brightly painted and cluttered with elaborately decorated statues. The greatest, the gold and ivory statue of Athena, 12m high, was taken to Constantinople in AD426 and melted down. A copy is in the National Archaeological Museum (see page 42). The marble friezes which adorned the Parthenon and Temple of Athena Nike were removed by Lord Elgin, British ambassador to the Ottoman Sultan, in 1801, and are in the British Museum. Greeks strongly resent this and demand their return.

In the Middle Ages the Parthenon was used as a Christian church, and in 1466 it became a Turkish mosque. The Turks later used it as a powder magazine.

Propylaea (Propylaia)

The Propylaia, the dramatic gateway to the Acropolis temple complex, combined Ionic and Doric features. Built between 437 and 432BC by the architect Mnesikles, its 46m-wide portico was pierced by five elaborate gates. The north wing of the Propylaia housed the Pinakotheke, which was built in the 5th century BC as a portrait gallery. The Pinakotheke was in use as a powder magazine when it was struck by lightning in 1645. It has been partly restored.

The Sacred Way

After entering the temple site by the Propylaia, worshippers passed along the flag-stoned Sacred Way, lined with statues of deities and heroes, to the Parthenon, pausing to worship at one or all of the shrines on the way. There are fine views of Athens from here.

The south portico of the Erechtheion, the holiest shrine of the Acropolis temple complex

CLASSICAL ARCHITECTURE

The temples of ancient Greece still have the power to move the visitor after two and a half millennia – an amazing tribute to their builders. The architects of classical Greece picked the setting for each temple as carefully as they planned its proportions. Besotted with the possibilities of geometry, they strove for simplicity, harmony and balance through a complex series of interrelated ratios. Few designers in the intervening centuries have matched their talents.

The temples of the 6th and 5th centuries BC, the golden age of Greek architecture, were built to a strict pattern. Steps surrounded a rectangular stone platform which supported fluted columns topped by a gabled roof and decorated with elaborate friezes depicting gods, heroes and monsters.

Again and again, the builders managed the brilliant trick of making the massive marble columns seem light and delicate, balancing height against width and horizontal against vertical by the use of the simplest of harmonic ratios.

Doric temple architecture, originating in mainland Greece, was the earliest and plainest of the three 'orders' of classical architecture.

Above: Corinthian capital
Left: Corinthian columns of the Olympion Dhios

Columns had no base, a simple capital at the top, and no more than 20 flutes or decorative grooves. Doric temples, like the superbly preserved Temple of Apollo at Vassai, can appear more massive than those built in the Ionian style. The Parthenon, finest of all the Doric buildings, avoids this by sleight

of hand: its columns slope slightly inward for strength, and the corner columns, which should appear larger than the others, are in fact slightly smaller, tricking the eye into seeing a larger space.

The Ionic style originated among the Greek cities of the Asia Minor coast. Ionic columns have a subdivided base, a shaft with 20 flutes, a decorated capital, and are often slimmer than the Doric column. The later Corinthian style, developed after the Roman conquest of Greece, is a fusion of Greek and Roman design. Base and shaft are similar to Ionic columns, while the cup-shaped capital is more floridly carved with leaves and garlands.

AROUND THE ACROPOLIS

ACROPOLIS INTERPRETATION CENTRE

Copies of the friezes from the Parthenon, including those in the British Museum and the Acropolis Museum, are the main attractions of this new centre for conservation and restoration. Copies of sculptures from the Erechtheion and Temple of Athena Nike will also be displayed, and it is planned to relocate the Acropolis Museum to a new building next to the Centre.

2–4 Makriyianni (Makrigiani) (tel: 9239 381). Open: Monday to Friday, 9am–2pm; Monday, Wednesday and Friday, also 6pm–8pm; weekends, 10am–2pm. Admission free.

LOFOS FILOPAPOU (Hill of the Muses)

Named after the Roman consul Philopappos, the hill is topped by his 12m-high monumental tomb, built in AD116. Around it are the remnants of 3rd-century BC fortifications.

ODION IRÓDOU ATTIKO (Odeon of Herod Atticus)

Built into the rock of the Acropolis in AD161, this huge theatre is the main venue for the annual Athens Festival of music, theatre and dance. It seats 6,000, and its superb acoustics carry voices to the highest of its many tiers of seats.

The theatre's well-preserved Roman façade with its tiers of arches can be viewed from the stepped path to the Acropolis, which runs past it.

*Dhionissou Areopayitou. Open: for performances only (see **Entertainment**, page 149).*

OLYMPION DHIOS AND PÍLI ADHRIANOÚ (Olympion Zeus and Arch Of Hadrian)

The temple of Olympian Zeus was one of the ancient world's greatest, completed by the Roman Emperor Hadrian in AD132. It measured 107.45m by 41m. Only 15 of its 84 columns still stand, the rest having been taken by successive occupiers of Athens, including Genoese, Venetians and Turks, for building stone.

Next to the Temple of Olympian Zeus, the monumental arch divided Hadrian's new Roman city from older Hellenic Athens.

Junction of Leoforos Singrou and Leoforos Amalias (tel: 9226 330). Open: daily, except Monday, 8.30am–3pm. Admission charge.

Arch of Hadrian

Only 15 of the original columns of the Temple of Olympian Zeus still stand

PNYX

On this low hill west of the Acropolis the Athenian popular assembly met until the late 4th century BC, when it relocated to the Théatro Dhionissou (Theatre of Dionysos) below the Acropolis. There is little to see during the day, but during the summer the Pnyx is the venue for the nightly Sound and Light show telling the story of the Acropolis (see **Entertainment**, page 153).

THEATRO DHIONISSOU
(Theatre of Dionysos)

The oldest of the buildings on the southern slope of the Acropolis, the 17,000-seat theatre with its 67 tiers of seats is separated from the Odeon of Herod Atticus by the sites of the Sanctuaries of Asklepios and of Dionysos Eleutheros, of which only two Corinthian columns remain. Built in the 4th century BC, the theatre was embellished and enlarged in the 1st century AD under the Roman emperor Nero, with the addition of elaborately carved front-row seats for the priests of Dionysos and other dignitaries.

Next to the theatre are the remains of two sanctuaries to Asklepios, god of healing, dating from the 4th and 5th centuries BC, and the rows of column bases which mark the site of the 2nd-century BC Stoa of Eumenes.
Dhionissou Areopayitou (tel: 3224 625). Open: daily, 8.30am–2.30pm.

Tiers of seats ring the auditorium of the Theatre of Dionysos

NORTH OF THE ACROPOLIS

AGORÁ (Ancient Market-place)

This was the heart of everyday life in ancient Athens and after the Acropolis is the most important and evocative of the city's ancient sites. Highlights include the 5th-century BC Thission, the most intact of all Greece's temples. So called because its friezes (now badly damaged) showed the exploits of Theseus, the building with its 34 Doric columns was a temple to Ifestos (Hephaestos), the armourer of the gods and the deity of smiths and artisans.

Rebuilt after the Persian invasion of 480BC, the Agorá was ringed by long, colonnaded buildings called *stoas*. One of these, the 2nd-century BC Stoa Attalou (Stoa of Attalos II), was rebuilt by American archaeologists. A striking two-storey building with a Doric colonnade on the ground floor and an Ionic one above, it is now the Mousío

A tombstone at the Keramikos cemetery shows an Athenian noble family

Agorá (Agorá Museum), with a collection of vases and fragmented statues.

Just below the upper entrance to the site stands the Byzantine church of Ayioi Apostoloi, built in the 11th century AD on a site on which St Paul is said to have preached.

Main entrance is on Adhrianoú (tel: 3210 185), 5 minutes walk from Monastiráki metro station. Open: daily, except Monday, 8.30am–2.45pm. Admission charge.

ÁRIOS PÁGOS (Areopagus)

According to legend it was on this rocky hilltop above the site of the ancient Agorá that Ares the war god was tried by the other Olympians for the murder of one of the sons of Poseidon. A cave in the hillside was the Sanctuary of the Eumenides (the Harpies), who were goddesses of revenge. The summit offers views of the Ancient Agorá and the Acropolis.

KERAMIKOS CEMETERY AND MUSEÍO

The cemetery of ancient Athens was excavated in the 19th century, revealing rows of *stelae* (tombstones) of the Athenian élite. Others are on show in the small museum and in the National Archaeological Museum (see page 42). *Ermou 148 (tel: 3463 552). Open: daily, except Monday, 8.30am–3pm.*

NÁOS EÓLOU
(Tower of the Winds)

Overlooking the Roman Forum, this 13m-high octagonal marble building was built in the 1st century AD. The tower takes its name from the winged figures carved on each face to represent the winds, and housed a water-clock for those using the nearby Forum.

The Tower of the Winds and columns of the Roman market-place

Near junction of Eólou and Adhrianoú, opposite Romaiki Agorá. Not open to the public.

ROMAIKI AGORÁ (Roman Forum)

The site of the Roman market-place, which complemented the nearby Ancient Agorá, is marked by the massive four-columned gateway built in the 2nd century AD. There is little else to see within the site.

Pelopida and Eólou (tel: 3245 220). Open: daily, except Monday, 8.30am–2.45pm. Admission charge.

LIFE IN THE MARKET-PLACE

The Ancient Agorá and the later Forum were more than just places to buy and sell goods and services. The long porches of the *stoas* surrounding them provided shelter for philosophers and politicians as well as for traders. Below the Thission stood the government buildings of Ancient Athens. The city's 500 magistrates met in the Bouleuterion, and 50 of them lived in rotation for one month of the year in the circular Tholos next to it. The Metroon, built in the 2nd century BC, was both a ' temple and a state library.

The ancient Agorá in Athens, once the social and commercial hub of the city

MODERN ATHENS

The main thoroughfares, squares and public buildings of modern Athens date from the 19th century, when Otho I, first king of independent Greece, decreed a new capital among the ancient ruins. Sadly, much of Otho's gracious little capital was destroyed during World War II, and post-war development has swamped the rest.

ETHNIKÓS KÍPOS
(National Gardens)
Laid out for Otho I's queen, Amalia, by a Bavarian landscape architect, the former garden of the Anáktora (Royal Palace, now the Voulí, the Parliament Building) is the only large green space in central Athens. A band plays at its open-air café on summer evenings.
The entrance gates are on Amalias, Iródou and Vasilissis Sofias. Open: sunrise to sunset. Admission free.

KOLONAKI
The smartest shops, nightspots and restaurants in Athens are in this fashionable suburb on the slopes of Likavitós, 10 minutes' walk from Sindagma. The centre of Kolonaki is Platia Kolonaki, a central square ringed by chic cafés and piano bars. Behind it, steep streets and steps climb the hill.

LIKAVITÓS
This wooded 227m-high peak topped by the chapel of Ayios Yioryios (St George) is a prominent landmark, from which there are fine views of the Acropolis, the city and its surroundings. A path leads to the chapel from the Hotel St George-Lykabettos, Kleomenous 2. The lazy way is to take the funicular, also from Kleomenous.

MITROPÓLIS (Cathedral)
The massive and ugly new cathedral, built in the 19th century, dwarfs the much prettier late 12th-century building next to it, uniquely built of fragments from ancient temples and medieval buildings. Many of the ancient fragments have had crosses carved on them later. *Platia Mitropólis.*

OMONIA
Platia Omonia, at the opposite end of Stadhiou from Sindagma, is the city's other main square. Once elegant, it has become a busy traffic and public transport hub with little of its former charm.

PIRAIÉVS (Piraeus)
The port of Athens, west of the city, is connected to it by a single metro line. You will have to pass through the harbour district to visit the islands of the Argolikós-Saronikós Kólpos (Argo-Saronic Gulf) (see Getting Away From it All, pages 134–5), though many of the excursion boats now leave from Faliron Bay to the west of Piraeus.

MIKROLIMANO (Little Harbour)
Sometimes called Turkolimano (Turkish

The whitewashed chapel of Ayios Yioryios on Likavitós

Harbour), Mikrolimano is between Piraeus itself and Faliron. This lagoon-like one-time fishing harbour is now filled with yachts but is still surrounded by the best fish restaurants in Athens, almost two dozen of them.

PLAKA

Below the Acropolis, on its north and east sides, the old-fashioned streets of the Plaka with their tall, stucco-fronted houses and occasional gardens full of palms or lemon trees are the prettiest part of Athens. There are few cars and plenty of shops, cafés, restaurants and leafy squares. Tourism plays a big role, but has not yet taken over the Plaka completely. The main shopping street is Adhrianoú, running around the northwest edge of the Plaka.

Brightly painted houses like this 19th-century mansion are typical of the old Plaka

SINDAGMA

Platia Sindagma is the heart of modern Athens, surrounded by expensive hotels, banks and airline offices, and open-air cafés. The meeting-point of the city's main avenues – Ermou, Amalias, Stadhiou and Venizelou (also called Panepisthimiou) – Sindagma is an island in a sea of traffic. The drills and diggers at work on the new Athens underground system (scheduled for completion by the end of the century) somewhat detract from its undoubted appeal.

STADION (Stadium)

This copy in marble of the ancient Stadium, built in stone in 330BC and rebuilt in marble in AD140, dates from the late 19th century. It was donated to the Greek people by the millionaire George Averof in time for the first modern Olympic Games in 1896.
Junction of Vasileos Konstandinou and Iródou Attikou. Open for events only.

VOULÍ (Parliament)

Borrowing the name of the ancient Athenian citizens' council, the Voulí is the most imposing of the city's 19th-century buildings. Built in 1843 as the palace of Otho I, the building and the Tomb of the Unknown Soldier outside it are guarded by white-kilted élite soldiers of the Evzones regiment.
Leoforos Amalias, east side of Syntagma. Not open to the public. Changing of the guard, 11am on Sundays.

ZÁPPION

This elegant cream-and-yellow building standing in formal gardens is the epitome of the neo-classical style popular in the reign of Otho I. Its most noteworthy feature is its mock-Corinthian portico. Completed in 1883, it was the gift to the city of millionaire Constantine Zappas, and is now a conference centre.
Located within the National Gardens. Open: sunrise to sunset.

MUSEUMS OF ATHENS

ETHNIKÍ PINAKOTHÍKI
(National Art Gallery)
Three paintings by El Greco (born in
Venetian-ruled Crete though he worked
in Spain) are the jewels of the gallery's
collection. Most of its other paintings are
by 19th-century Romantics.
Vasileos Konstandinou 50 (tel: 8217 717).
Open: Monday to Saturday, 9am–3pm;
Sunday, 10am–2pm. Admission charge.

ISTORIKO MOUSÍO
(National Historical Museum)
This contains an exhibition of paintings,
engravings, weapons and relics devoted
to the Greek struggle for independence
from the Middle Ages to the 20th
century.
Stadhiou 13 (tel: 3237 617). Open:
Tuesday to Friday, 9am–1.30pm; Saturday
and Sunday, 9am–12.30pm. Closed
Monday. Admission charge.

MOUSÍO ATHINON
(Athens Museum)
For a glimpse of Athens during its 19th-
century revival, visit the former royal
palace where a collection of paintings
and exhibits is housed in one of the
prettiest of the city's surviving neo-
classical buildings.
Paparigopoulou 7 (tel: 3246 164). Open:
Monday, Wednesday, Friday and
Saturday, 9am–1.30pm. Admission charge.

MOUSÍO BENÁKI
(Benaki Museum)
This cramped but fascinating collection
of Byzantine and Asian jewellery, icons
and textiles and colourful displays of
Greek national costume was closed in
1993 for refurbishment; its re-opening
date is uncertain.

Koumbari and Vasilissis Sofias
(tel: 3611 617).

MOUSIO ELLINIKIS LAOGRAFIAS
(Museum of Greek Folk Art)
Here you will find an eye-catching
collection of delicate embroideries and
magnificent clerical robes, and
traditional pottery from the islands.
Kidhathineon 17 (tel: 3229 031). Open:
daily, except Monday, 10am–2pm.
Admission charge.

MOUSÍO ETHNIKÓ ARKHEOLOGIKÓ
(National Archaeological Museum)
Whatever you do in Athens, do not miss
the finest museum in Greece, where
treasures from the royal tombs of
Mycenae compete for your attention
with the magnificent statue of Poseidon
and other bronzes, classical sculpture,
ceramics and statuettes. It is well worth
devoting most of a day to the huge
collection. If you try to rush round, you
will miss some of the most striking
highlights.

    Top billing goes to the Mycenaean
collection (Room 4), where pride of
place is given to the dazzling golden
'Mask of Agamemnon'. Now known to
belong to an earlier era than Homer's
hero, its age and sheer beauty make a
double impact. Around it are crammed
cases of glittering
Mycenaean
jewellery and
flowing frescos
from the palace
at Tiryns.

Bronze head in the
National Archaeological
Museum

The best way to view the breathtaking sculpture which is exhibited in the other halls of the ground floor is to begin at Room 7, left of the main entrance, and work your way round room by room. This way you get a tour in time from the earliest archaic *kouroi* (statues of graceful youths) through to the perfectly poised, mid-5th-century BC statue of Posiedon, found on the seabed off Évvoia about 70 years ago.

The first floor houses the Helen Stathatos collection of gold funerary decorations. The richly decorated black-and-red figure vases from the 6th and 5th century BC on the second floor afford fascinating glimpses of everyday life among the ancient temples and palaces.

Patission 44 (tel: 8217 717). Open: Monday, 10.30am–5pm; Tuesday to Sunday, 8am–5pm. Admission charge.

MOUSÍO GOULANDRI KIKLÁDHIKI TEXNI
(Goulandris Museum of Cycladic and Ancient Greek Art)
More than 200 startlingly modern-looking statuettes, tools, weapons and ceramics from the Cycladic civilisation which dominated Greece between 3000 and 2000BC are displayed here.

Neofytou Douka 4 (tel: 7234 931). Open: Monday to Wednesday and Friday, 10am–4pm; Saturday, 10am–1pm. Admission charge.

MOUSÍO KANELLÓPOULOS
(Kanelloupoulos Museum)
Feast your eyes here on glowing Byzantine icons, jewellery, and traditional weavings, furniture and embroidery in a 19th-century Plaka mansion.

Corner of Theorias and Panos (tel: 3212

The Goulandris Museum

313). Open: daily, except Monday, 8.30am–3pm. Admission charge.

POLEMIKO MOUSÍO
(War Museum)
Housed in an ugly 1960s block, this museum was created by the Colonels' junta to glorify the army. It offers an insight into Greece's deep vein of patriotism, fostered by struggles against so many invaders, but the antique aircraft which sit outside and the collections of obsolete weapons and battle tableaux within are not very exciting.

Vasilissis Sofias and Rizari (tel: 7290 543). Open: daily, except Monday, 9am–2pm. Admission free.

VIZANDINÓ MOUSÍO
(Byzantine Museum)
Icons are the chief glory of this collection, though the best-known exhibit is the Epitaphios of Thessaloníki, a 14th-century embroidery depicting the Lamentation.

Vasilissis Sofias 22 (tel: 7231 570). Open: daily, except Monday, 8.30am–3pm. Admission charge.

The Plaka and the Acropolis

The Plaka is the most picturesque part of Athens and alone of the older districts has survived fairly intact. Its narrow streets offer an escape from the manic Athens traffic. *Allow up to 4 hours.*

Start at Monastiráki metro station and head down Ifaistou (Ifestou) into the Flea Market, a mix of jewellers, souvenir shops, shoemakers, boutiques, and army surplus stores.

1 PLATIA AVISSINIAS

About 5 minutes' walk from Monastiráki, turn away from the boutiques and souvenir shops of Ifaistou for a look at an old-fashioned clutter of furniture-makers, antique stalls and street vendors selling junk of all kinds.

At the end of Ifaistou turn left then left again on to Adhrianou.

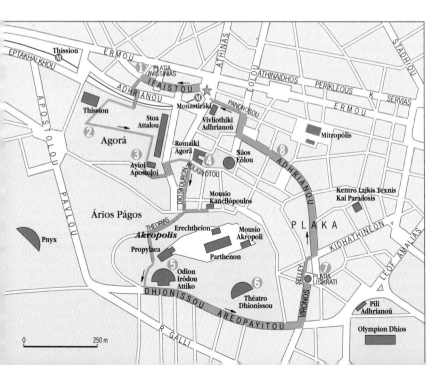

2 ANCIENT AGORÁ

Entering the Agorá by its lower gate, follow the signs to the Thission for one of the best views in Athens. Most of the modern city is hidden. Mount Imittós dominates the eastern skyline with the wooded slopes of Ários Págos to the south, and above them the crag of the Acropolis and the pillars of the Parthenon. As a bonus, the whole of the Agorá, the heart of the ancient city, is laid out in front of you (see page 38).

3 AYIOI APOSTOLOI

Before leaving the Agorá by the upper gate, pause to look at the domed Ayioi Apostoloi (Holy Apostles), a Byzantine church dating from the 11th century and built on a site where St Paul is said to have preached.

Leaving the Agorá, turn left and left again, and then right on to Polignotou.

4 ROMAIKI AGORÁ (THE ROMAN AGORÁ)

A four-columned portico marks the entrance to the site of the Roman Agorá. To the north stands the site of the Vivliothiki Adhrianoú (currently closed for excavation). On the east side of the site stands Náos Eólou (Tower of the Winds). Built in the 1st century BC, it was a combined sundial and water-clock.

Turn right on Dioskouron, a steep street of old-fashioned, yellow-painted stucco houses which becomes a flight of steps before it joins Theorias.

Turn right to go direct to the Acropolis or detour left for 50m to visit the Mousío Kanellópoulos (Kanelloupoulos Museum, signposted, see pages 42–3).

Theorias runs above the Ancient Agorá, passes between the Acropolis and the Ários Págos and curves left to the entrance to the Acropolis (see pages 32–3).

The uphill part of the walk ends here. From the Acropolis take the stepped path downhill through pine trees for about 100m and turn left.

5 ODION IRÓDOU ATTIKO (ODEON OF HEROD ATTICUS)

This fine Roman theatre was built in AD161. Athens Festival events are staged here in summer. It is open only for performances (see page 36).

Descend a short flight of steps to emerge on to busy Dhionissou Areopayitou. Turn left and walk downhill for 200m past the Theatre of Dionysus.

6 THÉATRO DHIONISSOU (THEATRE OF DIONYSUS)

The works of the great Athenian playwrights were first performed in this theatre, which dates from about 534BC (see page 37).

At the foot of Dhionissou Areopayitou, turn left on to Vironos and follow it to Platia Lisikrati.

7 PLATIA LISIKRATI

Marked by the 4th-century BC Lysikrates Monument whose six Corinthian half-columns commemorate a prizewinning *choregos* (choirmaster), this is a good place to stop for a drink or a meal.

Vironos leads on to Selley. At its end, turn right then immediately left, back on to Adhrianoú.

8 SHOPPING ON ADHRIANOÚ AND PANDROSOU

Adhrianoú is lined with shops selling pottery, clothes, and brightly coloured rugs and carpets.

Turn right on to Eólou, then left on to Pandrosou. This 'new' flea-market street with its dozens of souvenir shops leads back to Monastiráki.

Attikí

(Attica)

*A*ttica is the mythic heartland of ancient Greece and it takes only a little while to escape from Athens to the little-changed landscape of the Messogia, in the midst of the southern peninsula. Covered with vineyards and olive groves as it has been since antiquity, the region produces much of the *retsina* drunk in Athenian tavernas.

On the southern tip of the peninsula, the columns of the Temple of Poseidon, dramatically silhouetted against the sunset, are one of the great sights. Other delightful temples are to be seen at Vravróna and Thorikón (Thorikos), on the peninsula's east coast.

A string of fashionably casual seaside suburbs, beaches and marinas on the west coast of the Attica peninsula attracts droves of Athenians in summer. The best sandy beaches, though, are on the bay of Marathón, 42km from Athens, where a mound and a modern monument mark the grave of the Athenians who fell in

battle against the Persians in 490BC. Northwest of Athens, grim fortresses and other ghostly battlefields mark the one-time frontier of Athens with Thebes, its rival, while the fortresses of Aigósthena, Elevtherai, and Plataiaí, mark where the Spartans, Athenians and their allies again defeated the Persians in 479.

West of Athens, the coastal highway to Corinth passes through industrial suburbs which generate much of the capital's notorious smog.

The ruins of Eleusis, once one of the most important religious shrines in Greece

The Temple of Themis (goddess of Justice) at Rhamnoós, destroyed by the Persians

ATTICA

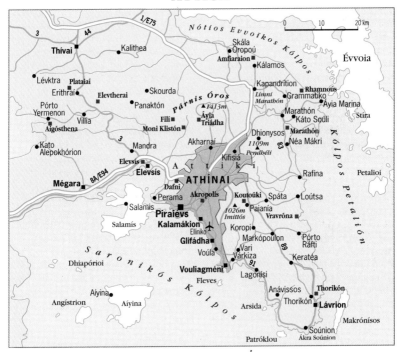

The Temple of Poseidon at Cape Soúnion, the southern tip of Attica

THE PLAYGROUND OF ATHENS: AKTÍ APOLLONA (APOLLO COAST)

South of Athens lie the city's seaside suburbs and marinas, offering Athenians a summer getaway. Pollution is a problem on beaches closer to the busy harbour of Piraiévs (Piraeus), and swimming between Piraeus and Glifádha is not recommended. Beyond this, a string of clean beaches extends along the west-facing Aktí Apollona (Apollo Coast) to the tip of the peninsula.

AKRA SOÚNION (CAPE SOÚNION)

After the Acropolis, the **Temple of Poseidon** in silhouette against the sunset is the best-known and most striking image of Attica. Perched 60m above the sea on the peninsula's southern tip, the temple was built between 444 and 440BC and dedicated to Poseidon. It was restored after independence in the 19th century, 16 Doric columns of the original 34 surviving. Just 6.10m high, the columns seem taller because of their slimness, measuring only 1m in diameter at the base and 0.79m at the top. On one of the two columns of the entrance portico is carved the name of Lord Byron, who visited the temple in 1810.

The temple is at its most spectacular at sunset, when it is also at its most crowded as dozens of sightseeing coaches arrive from Athens.

Temple of Poseidon, 70km south of Athens (tel: 0292 39363). Open: Monday to Saturday, 9am–sunset; Sunday, 10am–sunset. Admission charge.

GLIFÁDHA (GLYFADHA)

The best swimming near Athens is at Glyfadha , the smart suburb 18km from the city centre, favoured by wealthy Athenians and expatriates. There is a clean beach operated by the National Tourist Organisation, a marina, and the capital's only 18-hole golf course (see Sports, page 162).

KOUTOÚKI CAVE

The Koutoúki Cave, discovered in 1926,

plunges into the side of Imittós. Within, water trickles down floodlit rose-coloured walls and needle-sharp stalactites.

4km from the village of Paianía (Peania) and 18km from Athens (tel: 6642 910). Open: Tuesday to Sunday, 8.30am–3pm. Admission charge.

VARI

Vari comes to bubbling life after dark, when it is a favourite dinner destination for Athenians. Waiters dressed in the baggy pants and embroidered waistcoats of traditional costume drum up business for dozens of rival restaurants. Not for vegetarians or the faint-hearted, Vari's taverns cater to serious carnivores with dishes like whole lamb on the spit, skewered meat, *kokoretsi* (spit-roasted lamb entrails) and sheep's brains.
27km from Athens.

VÁRKIZA

A lively resort and fishing harbour, Várkiza has a 750m stretch of sand with facilities operated by the National Tourist Organisation. Cafés and expensive restaurants surround its small port and many Athenians drive out for the evening, especially at weekends, to sample freshly caught seafood.
31km south of Athens.

VOULIAGMÉNI

The smartest of all the resort suburbs, Vouliagméni is the haunt of Athenian shipping millionaires and other tycoons, as can be seen from the luxury yachts and cruisers at anchor in its marina. Villas and hotels are dotted among the pine trees of two wooded headlands

The richly stocked yacht marina in the fashionable Athenian suburb of Glyfadha

> **ANCIENT ATTICA**
> Theseus, the mythical king who slew the Minotaur and thus freed Athens from paying tribute to the Minoan rulers of Knossos, united the petty kingdoms of Attica with Athens. Throughout ancient times the region remained part of the Athenian city-state, providing Athens with wine, bread, olives, marble for its great temples and silver from the Lavrion mines. During the Peloponnesian War of the 5th century BC, Sparta struck at Athens by invading Attica each year, systematically felling its olive groves and cutting off the city's food supply.
>
> With the decline of Athens, Attica declined too and as Christianity took over its temples fell into disuse, to be rediscovered only in the 19th century.

framing Vouliagméni's natural harbour. Vouliagméni's beaches and luxury hotels are popular and crowded in summer.
24km south of Athens.

MARATHÓN AND THE EAST COAST

AMFIARAION

Located in a peaceful, pine-covered gully, rows of stone coffins and statue pedestals give a clear picture of the layout of the ancient site, a sanctuary dedicated to the legendary Amphiaraos, king of Argos, and dating from the 4th century BC. The lion-footed seats of the priests in the front row of its 3,000-seat theatre are well preserved.

On the Kálamos road, 38km north of Athens. Open: Monday to Friday, 8am–6pm; weekends, 8.30am–3pm. Admission charge.

MARATHÓN

The name is legendary but there is little to see at Marathón. The only relic of the battle is the 12m-high mound marking the tomb of the 192 Athenians who fell. It stands among citrus groves behind a 2km crescent of sandy beach. The mound of the Plataians, allies of Athens, is 5km away on the opposite (inland) side of the main road near the small village of Vranas. Next to it, the Marathón Archaeological Museum houses finds from the tomb, gravestones and carvings from the mid-4th century

The burial mound at Marathón, beneath which archaeologists found bones of the Athenian dead

BC, pottery and stone tools from the Cycladic and Mycenaean eras, and an Egyptian-style *kouros* from the 2nd century BC. In the adjacent Bronze Age tomb, 10 skeletons dating from the 2nd millennium BC are open to view.

Tomb and museum (tel: 0294 55155), 42km from Athens and 5km from the resort of Marathón. Open: daily, except Monday, 8.30am–3pm. Admission charge.

RAFÍNA

Ferries and hydrofoils to the Aegean islands lend an air of bustle to this small port. Its half-moon harbour front is packed with excellent fish tavernas, a lovely place for a night out. In the

---

THE BATTLE OF MARATHÓN

With its long sweep of gently shelving beach the bay of Marathónas is the perfect place for a seaborne invasion, and it was here in 490BC that the Persian general Mardonios landed with a fleet and an army of perhaps 30,000. They were met by 10,000 Athenians and their Plataian allies. Though heavily outnumbered, the Athenians charged the Persians and routed them. The Athenian historians claimed only 192 of their citizen soldiers were killed (among them the Athenian commander Kallimakhos) for 6,400 Persian dead. Miltiades, the surviving commander, sent a runner to tell the city of the victory. He ran non-stop, gasping out his news before dying of exhaustion and inspiring the modern marathon event, run over a course which corresponds to the distance from the battlefield to the city of Athens.

Temple of Artemis at Vravróna, possibly founded by Iphigenia, daughter of Agamemnon. Beyond the temple foundations are the dining rooms and dormitories of the young priestesses that served here

daytime, Evia and the slopes of Oxi Oros tantalise on the horizon.

40km east of Athens

RHAMNOÓS (RAMNOUS)

Ramnous is now off the beaten track, but in ancient times it controlled all the shipping passing through the Gulf of Evia. The most impressive part of the site, the 4th-century BC fortified harbour, is closed for further archaeological work. The site is famous for its Temple of Nemesis, the goddess of justice, retribution and atonement (build about 435BC), the only such temple known outside Asia Minor, and the Temple of Themis, the goddess of world order (built about 500BC).

Káto Soúli (tel: 0294 63477), 55km northeast of Athens; follow signs from main Marathón road. Open: Monday to Saturday, 7am–6pm; Sunday, 8am–6pm. Admission charge.

THORIKÓN (THORIKOS)

A short distance from the ugly mining town of Lávrion, close to Attica's southern tip, ancient Thorikos is still being excavated. Quite densely populated from 2900BC onwards, the town became a Mycenaean stronghold, and three 16th-century BC beehive graves have been discovered. Its most interesting feature is an unusual 4th-century BC oval-shaped theatre with tiers of seats for 5,000 spectators. Little remains of the site's acropolis or other buildings.

Signposted 'Theatre Antique' from Lávrion. Free access.

VRAVRÓNA (BRAURON)

Here you will find a cluster of graceful temple columns among vineyards and reedbeds. The earliest finds from the site are from as early as 1700BC, but the main ruins are those of the 5th-century BC Temple of Artemis, the goddess of female chastity, a cult which goes back to the 9th century BC. A small museum exhibits jewellery and sacred vessels from the temple. More interesting are the lively statues of the *arktoi* or 'bear-maidens' who were the priestesses of Artemis. The 15th-century AD chapel of Ayios Yioryios, within the temple precinct, has some interesting remains of frescos.

Vravróna Archaeological Site (tel: 0299 27020), on the road to Pórto Ráfti, 7km from Markópoulon, signposted. Open: daily, except Monday, 8.30am–3pm. Admission charge.

The east coast harbour of Rafina is Attica's gateway to the islands

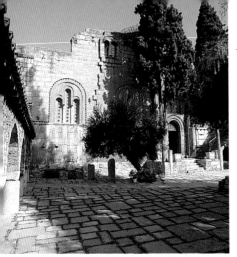

The courtyard at the Dafni Monastery. The church interior is a treasure house of mid-Byzantine mosaics – even after Turkish troops attempted to melt the gold out of the fragments

NORTHERN ATTIKA

DAFNÍ MONASTERY

The monastery and church of the Virgin at Dafní date from the 11th century AD, though there has been a monastery on the site since the 6th century. Much of the splendid gold mosaic of the interior survives; its most striking feature is the mosaic of a characteristically stern-looking, Byzantine-style Christ, though the other portraits are very human, lively and almost classical in their rendering. The exterior, with its graceful arcade and portico using columns and fragments lifted from an earlier temple of Apollo, is less stolid than many modern Orthodox churches and is a typical Byzantine mix of brickwork and masonry.

Signposted off the main Athens-Eleusis-Corinth highway, 11km from the centre of Athens (tel: 5811 558). Open: daily, 8.30am–3pm. Admission charge.

ELEVSÍS (ELEUSIS)

Set on a low hill overlooking the sea and surrounded by refineries and factories,

---

DEMETER AND AND PERSEPHONE

Persephone, daughter of Zeus and Demeter, goddess of the earth's fruits, was carried off by Hades (to whom Zeus had promised Persephone in marriage) to the underworld. During her search for her daughter, Demeter came to Eleusis where she gave the king permission to build a temple in her honour. To this she retired, vowing that until Persephone was returned she would neither reside in Olympus nor allow crops to grow on earth.

Zeus relented, commanding Hades to return Persephone. To this Hades consented but he gave Persephone part of a pomegranate to eat. Having eaten in the underworld she was bound to return there, and was allowed to live on the earth with her mother only between sowing time in the autumn and harvest in early summer. The hot, arid summer months she spent underground as 'goddess of the dead'. Demeter and Persephone were worshipped together as goddesses of growth, especially of cultivated grain.

Eleusis is now an unprepossessing place but it was one of the great sanctuaries of ancient times. Dedicated to the fertility goddesses Persephone and Demeter, the site was rediscovered and excavated in the 19th century. Roman ruins overlay the earlier Greek temple. Its main features are the great forecourt and entrance to the sanctuary built by the Romans in the 2nd century AD, the Telesterion, which was the centre of the sanctuary, and the classical-era defensive

walls around the site.
Eleusís Archaeological Site (tel: 5546 019), signposted from the main Athens-Eleusís-Corinth highway, 26km northwest of Athens. Open: daily, except Monday, 8.30am–3pm. Admission charge.

ELEVTHERAI

This 4th-century BC Athenian fortress guards the pass between the Pateras and Kitheron ranges through which the former National Road between Athens and Thebes still runs. One massive wall of grey limestone blocks still stands, and goats shelter in the ruins of its towers.
Signposted to the north of the Athens–Thebes road, 1km north of the Pórto Germeno turning. Unenclosed.

PÓRTO YERMENO (PORTO GERMENO)

This delightful, quiet little resort at the head of an arm of the Korinthiakós Kólpos (Gulf of Corinth) seems more remote than it is. Ringed by steep, pine-covered slopes, it has a crescent of pebbly beach, busy only on summer weekends, and a handful of guesthouses and fish restaurants.
Signposted from Athens-Thebes highway, 71km northwest of Athens.

Nearby is the once-mighty Athenian fortress of Aigósthena, built in the 4th century BC as part of the defences on the Theban border. Its massive walls ring a low hilltop, and five of its 15 square towers are still standing.
500m from Pórto Germeno village. Unenclosed.

THÍVAI (THEBES)

A ruined 13th-century Frankish tower stands atop the hill which was the acropolis of ancient Thebes, one of the most powerful of the city-states. Allied with the Persians against Athens in 480BC, Thebes remained a rival until Sparta defeated Athens in the Peloponnesian War. Thebes' finest hour came in 371BC when it defeated Sparta to become chief of the Hellenic states. It was destroyed by Alexander in 336BC. The main point of interest today is the Mousio Thivai Arkheologiko (Thebes Archaeological Museum); the collection includes a 6th-century BC *kouros*, some unique black tombstones, and Mycenaean sarcophagi.
Thebes is 81km northwest of Athens. The Thebes Archaeological Museum (tel: 0262 27913) is next door to the castle. Open: daily, except Monday, 8.30am–3pm. Admission charge.

BATTLEFIELDS OF NORTHERN ATTICA

Three great battles for ancient Greece were fought in northern Attica. At Thermopylae (480BC), the pass connecting Attica and Thessaly, 300 Spartans under King Leonidas fought to the death against a much larger Persian force. They were avenged at Plataiaí (479BC) by a Greek alliance. At Lévktra (371BC) Thebes defeated mighty Sparta. There is little to see at the battlefields, but a statue of Leonidas stands near the site of Thermopylae, beside the OE1 highway.
Lévktra: 12km south of Thebes, signposted.
Plataiaí 17km south of Thebes, signposted.
Thermopylae: near Kamena Vourla on OE1 (National Road 1), signposted.

Attika and Ákra Soúnion

The best way to see the countryside and the superb archaeological sites of Attica is by car. The high point of the tour is the magnificent Temple of Poseidon at Ákra Soúnion (Cape Soúnion), on the very southern tip of the Attica peninsula. *Starting from central Athens, the tour distance is 180km. Allow 4 to 6 hours driving.*

Leave Athens by the main coast highway, passing through the seaside suburbs of Glifádha, Voúla and Vouliagméni. On a clear day the island of Aíyina can be seen to the west, and the waters of the Saronikós Kólpos (Saronic Gulf) are dotted with yachts and ferries.

At Várkiza, set on a scenic bay with a pay beach managed by the Greek National Tourist Organisation, turn inland, following the

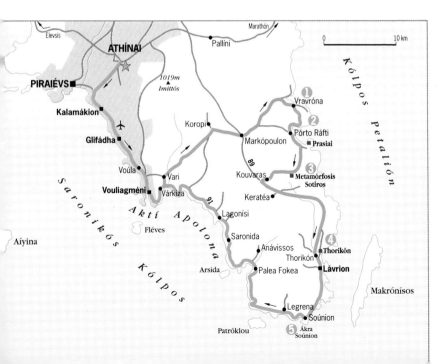

signs to *Vari (2km)*, then turn right in the direction of Koropi.

Leaving the urban sprawl of Athens, the countryside is much scarred by marble quarrying. At the Koropi crossroads, take the second right, signposted to Markópoulon, and drive through prettier surroundings of rolling hills dotted with olive trees and vineyards.

Mount Parnitha dominates the Athens skyline and offers escape from the summer heat

At Markópoulon, follow signs first to Vravróna to visit the ancient temple site and museum, then to Pórto Ráfti. The road crosses a fertile plain covered with vineyards which sell their produce to the Kourtaki retsina winery in Markópoulo. The green vines are all the more striking in contrast to the barren hillsides around them.

After 7km turn right, following signs to Vravróna and Pórto Ráfti. 250m from the turning you will see the columns of ancient Vravróna (see page 51) on the left.

1 VRAVRÓNA

The sanctuary was dedicated to the goddess Artemis and dates from the 5th century BC. The site is shared by a 6th-century AD Christian basilica and the 15th-century chapel of Ayios Yioryios.

From Vravróna the road climbs through pine woods, descending after 3km to the sea.

2 PÓRTO RÁFTI

The spectacularly located port and beach resort of Pórto Ráfti, on a broad, almost-enclosed blue bay, is a lovely place to stop for a snack and a swim.

Leaving Pórto Ráfti turn right (signposted to Kouvaras), and keep right. The road climbs through a pine-wooded valley.

3 MONASTERY OF METAMÓRFOSIS SOTIROS (METAMORPHOSIS SOTIROS)

The stately terracotta domes and bell towers of the monastery of Metamorphosis Sotiros (Transformation of the Saviour) stand guard over its olives and vines, surrounded by cypresses and palms.

The road zigzags through hills before joining the main road to Lávrion, which is soon bypassed as you press on to Cape Soúnion. Detour to the ancient site at Thorikón (signposted 'Theatre Antique' to the right of the road just before you enter Lávrion).

4 THORIKÓN (THORIKOS)

An unusual oval-shaped theatre seating 5,000 is currently being excavated at this hillside site, which dates from the 5th century BC.

5 CAPE SOÚNION

Homer's 'sacred headland' is crowned by the Temple of Poseidon, set atop 60m-high sea-cliffs, and one of the most spectacular of Greece's ancient sites. The islands of Makrónisos and Kea float on the eastern horizon. The temple was built between 444 and 440BC and restored in the 19th century, the clifftop position making it an invaluable vantage point in war and it was at one time fortified. It was built as a tribute to the sea god Poseidon at a time of growing Athenian naval power.

Head back to Várkiza and Athens by the winding corniche road which follows the bays and headlands of the Apollo Coast. The drive back takes around 1 hour.

Pelopónnisos

(The Peloponnese)

Separated from the northern mainland by the Korinthiakós Kólpos (Gulf of Corinth), the Peloponnese is rich in history and in natural beauty. Its coasts have some of Greece's longest sandy beaches and prettiest remote coves, its mountains offer unrivalled views, and it is dotted with ancient palaces, castles and fortresses spanning 5,000 years.

The Isthmus of Corinth connects the Peloponnese with the northern mainland, and is cut across by the Dióriga Korínthou (Corinth Canal). Much of the region is mountainous, with one mighty chain of peaks, culminating in the Taïyetos summit, running down the centre.

Nowhere else is Greece's many-layered history so clearly on show. The northeast corner of the region was the cradle of the Mycenaean civilisation

The Arcadian Gate at Ancient Messini stands as a testament to the monumental engineering skills of Sparta's great rival

celebrated by Homer. The classical and Hellenistic eras which followed are represented by Sparta, Corinth, Epídhavros and other sites.

The Byzantines built the fairy-tale castle of Mistra, above the Evrótas valley. Frankish princes left castles on a dozen hilltops. The Venetians fortified Návplion and Monemvasía and built grim strongholds at Methóni and Koróni. The Turks added yet another layer of history.

The Peloponnese is the birthplace of modern Greece. Here the War of Independence began in 1821, and here its fiercest battles were fought for

possession of castles built hundreds of years earlier. Together with Athens and the Sterea Ellas, the Peloponnese was the nucleus of the new Greek state established in 1830.

The north coast between Corinth and Patras is backed by steeply rising mountain slopes. West of Patras, the coast is dominated by long, sandy beaches. Inland, every pass through the mountains is guarded by a medieval castle or classical temple, but one of the magnets for visitors is the magical site of ancient Olympia.

Each of the three peninsulas has its own aura: Akritas, with its Venetian fortresses, Taínaron with its deserted towers and Maléa with its empty hillsides.

On the east coast, some charmingly remote towns, villages and untouched beaches are cut off from the hinterland of the Peloponnese by the bulk of Párnon Óros (Mount Parnon).

THE PELOPONNESE

The theatre at Epídhavros

THE ARGOLID

The Argolid is a blunt peninsula pointing southeast into the Aegean. The peninsula and the fertile plain at its landward end are rich in ancient and medieval sites.

There are beach resorts at Tolón, 4km from Návplion, and Portokhéli, on the peninsula's southern tip.

ÁRGOS

The oldest continuously inhabited town in Europe – it was founded in 2000BC – stands amid olive and citrus groves, a grid of modern buildings surmounted by Larissa Castle 300m above.

Kastro Larissis (Larissa Castle)

The 13th-century Frankish Kastro Larissis (Larissa Castle) is impressive from below and ghostly within, as only the outer walls and the shell of the inner keep survive, but there are fine views south down the east coast.

Access is from the west side of the crag, 5km from the town centre. Signposted. Unenclosed.

Mousio Arkheologikou (Archaeological Museum)

The museum contains minor finds from ancient Argos, including pottery, weapons and mosaics and a suit of 8th-century BC bronze armour.

Town centre (tel: 0751 28819). Open: daily, except Monday, 8.30am–3pm. Admission charge.

Impressive remains of the 2nd-century AD Roman baths are to be found, along with the ruins of the largest theatre in Greece (capacity 20,000), on Gounaris, the road to Tripoli.

EPÍDHAVROS

Set in a landscaped site among pines, the restored 4th-century BC theatre is the finest in Greece, seating 14,000 in 55 tiers, and is the main remnant of a sanctuary dedicated to Asklepios, the god of healing. Attending the theatre was thought to be beneficial to the spirit and the structure is still in use for the Epídhavros Festival from June to August

each year, when the ancient plays are brought to life by its magnificent acoustics – you can clearly hear someone speaking in a normal voice, or even tearing a sheet of paper, from the top row of seats almost 23m above the stage. Only foundations remain of other buildings, though some of the tiered seats of the stadium still survive.
Archaeological Site and Museum (tel: 0753 22009). 28km east of Návplion and 3km from the village of Ligoúrion (Lygourion). Open: Monday, 11am–5pm; Tuesday to Saturday, 8am–5pm; Sunday and holidays, 8.30am–3pm. Admission charge.

IRÉON (IREO)

Cyclopean blocks and column sections litter the site of the Sanctuary of Hera, the earth goddess of Argos. Tiers of walls and foundations give a clear view of the

The legendary wooden horse of Troy, visualised by a 19th-century artist

ground plan, but there are no signs to help make sense of the site, which is best appreciated from its highest point, the flagstoned floor of the 7th-century BC Doric Temple of Hera.
Ireo Archaeological Site, 2km north of Inaxon, signposted erratically. Open: daily, 8.30am–3pm. Admission charge.

HOMER'S HEROES

In one of the greatest stories ever told, the blind poet Homer wrote, probably in the 8th century BC, about events which were already far in the past. Homer drew on earlier folk tales for the basic plot and characters of his epics, the *Iliad* and the *Odyssey*, which deal with the 10-year siege of Troy, in Asia Minor, by a league of Mycenaean kings and princes from the Greek mainland and islands.

The war began when Paris, younger son of King Priam of Troy, ran off with the beautiful Helen, wife of King Menelaus of Sparta. Menelaus summoned his allies – the mighty warrior and commander Agamemnon, king of Mycenae; Nestor, wise old king of Pilos and a skilled charioteer; cunning Odysseus, ruler of Ithaca; and the invincible Achilles, dipped by his mother in a sacred spring to protect him against all weapons. Homer's *Iliad* deals with the last year of the siege during which Achilles was killed by an arrow which pierced his ankle, his only vulnerable spot.

In the *Aeneid*, the Roman poet Virgil (70–19BC) tells how Troy fell not to the valour of Achilles but to a ruse. The Greeks built a giant wooden horse, which they left as an offering to Poseidon when the fleet sailed away. The Trojans dragged it into the city, not knowing that Greek warriors lurked within. That night, the fleet returned, the hidden commandos emerged to open the gates, and the city fell.

Top: the Lion Gate at Mycenae
Inset: Heinrich Schliemann

MIKÍNAI (MYCENAE)

The most impressive of the Argolid's dramatic ancient sites, excavated by the German Heinrich Schliemann (1822–90) in 1876s.

He first found the ramparts, then a circle of royal tombs. The corpses found in them were decked in golden masks (including the famous so-called 'Mask of Agamemnon') and bracelets, now in the National Archaeological Museum in Athens.

Pass through the ramparts by the Lion Gate with its carved lionesses. Immediately within, to the right, are the first tombs discovered, dating from the 16th century BC. Below these and outside the walls is a second tomb circle,

THE REAL MYCENAEANS

I have gazed upon the face of Agamemnon.
Heinrich Schliemann (1876)

In 1871 the German archaeologist Heinrich Schliemann staggered the world by finding proof that Homer's epics were more than myth. Inspired by the *Iliad*, he discovered the site of Troy near Canakkale in western Turkey. Three years later he made his first tentative excavations at Hycenae, and two years after that he uncovered the palace and tombs. In the tombs were gold-bedecked skeletons, one of them wearing the breathtaking golden mask now in the National Archaeological Museum in Athens. His discovery began an archaeologists' gold rush to excavate the rich sites surrounding Mycenae and ushered in a golden age of archaeological discovery.

The Mycenaeans were a Bronze-Age people who came to Greece from Asia around 2100BC, and over the next five centuries they created a world of tiny kingdoms ruled from hilltop palaces built of crude but imposing massive stone blocks. They settled throughout southern Greece and established colonies in the islands and overseas, trading with the great empires of Egypt and the Middle East and with the Minoans of Crete. This first Greek civilisation fell quite suddenly around 1200BC, leaving a treasury of finely detailed figurines of people, gods and animals in bronze, gold and ceramics, elaborate seals and frescos depicting scenes from everyday life, and gorgeous golden grave-goods. The later, Dorian Greeks, who settled among the mighty ruins of the Mycenaean civilisation, wove a tapestry of legend around the dimly remembered Mycenaeans and their palaces, kings and heroes.

excavated in 1951 and dating from the 17th century BC. Next to this is the so-called Tomb of Clytemnestra, a 14th-century BC domed royal grave. Above the tombs, the tiers of the Royal Palace are connected by zigzagging marble stairs rising to a fortified acropolis.

Opposite the main site is the splendid Treasury of Atreus, a 13th-century BC beehive tomb over 13m high quarried out of the hillside.

The site is 2km from modern Mikínai, 7km southeast of the main Corinth–Argos road. Signposted. Archaeological Site and Treasury of Atreus (tel: 0751 66585). Open: weekdays, 8.30am–5pm; weekends and holidays, 8.30am–3pm. Admission charge.

NÁVPLION

A delightfully pretty harbour town whose shuttered stucco façades date from Návplion's brief 19th-century moment of glory as free Greece's first capital.

Akronavplion (Its Kale)

A rugged ring of impressive Turkish–Venetian ramparts on the site of an earlier Frankish stronghold occupies a headland above the harbour. The Byzantine gatehouse has fine frescos dated to AD1291. The main area of the old citadel has now been converted into a hotel.

Bourtzi

A quaint miniature fortress built by the Venetians in 1471, with a six-sided tower, adorns the island in the middle of Návplion's harbour. It also served in the past as a prison and the local hangman's home, but is now deserted.

Palamidhi

Built on the heights between 1711 and 1714, when the town was Venice's regional capital, the imposing stronghold is entered through gateways bearing the Lion of St Mark. The view from the top is magnificent.

Palamidhi Fortress (tel: 0752 28036). Open: weekdays, 8am–5pm; weekends and holidays, 8.30am–3pm. Admission charge.

TIRYNS

'Cyclopean' limestone boulder walls, up to 7m high and 700m in circumference, led later Greeks to believe that this 13th-century BC stronghold was built not by men but by giants like the one-eyed Cyclops of the myths. It is, in fact, the finest surviving example of Mycenaean military architecture. Historians estimate that the original height of the walls may have been as much as 20m – they are 10m thick in places. Little is known of the builders or of the ruling family, but it is clear that the fortress suffered a violent end, the palace within being gutted by fire well before the classical period.

The fort is 4km north of Návplion (tel: 0752 22657). Open: weekdays, 8am–5pm; weekends and holidays, 8.30am–3pm. Admission charge.

The island fortress of Bourtzi guards the harbour at Návplion

DRAMA IN ANCIENT

The plays performed in theatres like Epídhavros were far more than mere entertainment. They began as religious experiences, and their purpose was to explain the ways of gods to men. They also, however, often commented on society and politics in the city. Later, the works of the great Greek dramatists influenced Roman theatre, and later still they inspired generation after generation of Western playwrights, including Shakespeare and his 16th- and 17th-century contemporaries. Modern theatre is still in their debt.

To the playwrights of ancient Athens, a comedy was more than merely a play to make people laugh, and a tragedy more than just a tear-jerker. Essentially, tragedy dealt with deeper religious or moral themes, and comedy with everyday affairs, but both forms were highly stylised and conventional. Actors were disguised in masks which portrayed their character's attributes and an on-stage chorus provided a running commentary.

Tragedies were presented in Athens at great annual festivals and were surrounded by splendid rituals. Every citizen (that is, every free-born Athenian man) was entitled and expected to attend.

Writers had a solemn social and religious responsibility and the most successful were richly rewarded.

Cutout: actor's mask

The plot was less important than the exposition of the dramatist's theme, since the audience was already familiar with the story-line. Athenian audiences, in particular, instead, wanted to see how a new play interpreted an old story, and one purpose of the drama was to keep alive tales which were a central part of Greek culture.

Though described as 'hard to analyse, impossible to translate', the ancient plays of writers like the tragedians Sophocles (496–406BC), Aeschylus (c.525–456BC) and Euripides (484–406BC), and the comedian

Cutout: actor's mask

Works of the great Greek dramatists were performed at the great Theatre of Epídhavros

GREECE

Aristophanes (448–380BC), are re-enacted each year at festivals in Athens and Epídhavros (see Entertainment, pages 148–49). These can be moving events, especially if you have an English translation of the script, and their themes and even their humour are as relevant and fresh today as when they were written.

Cutout: actor's mask

Actors preparing for a performance

ÁKRA AKRITAS
(CAPE AKRITAS)

ANÁKTORA NESTOROS
(Palace of Nestor)

It is hard to picture the 13th-century BC palace of the great elder statesman of the Trojan War from its mud and stone foundations, but the site has a fine view across Navarino Bay. There is a cavernous 13th-century BC beehive tomb about 100m from the palace site.
17km north of Pílos. Open: daily, except Monday, 8.30am–3pm. Admission charge.

Only the stone foundations of the Palace of Nestor survived a fire in the 12th century BC

KASTRO TON PARAMYTHION
(Castle of the Fairy-tales)

Winged horses, 5m-high stucco statues and tableaux from Greek history surround the extraordinary three-storey folly with its red and yellow spires and white plaster battlements built in the 1950s by the late Dr Haralambos Fournarakis.
On the shore, between Kiparissía and Filiatrá. From Kiparissía, follow signs to Agrili. The building is not open to the public.

The Castle of the Fairy-tales, a unique and colourful Greek folly

KIPARISSÍA

A pocket-sized Byzantine castle sits crumbling on a pine-covered hilltop above this farming and fishing town which spreads between the coastal hills and a long strip of pebbly beach.
1km from town centre.

KORÓNI

The lovely castle at Koróni looks east to the summits of Taïyetos (Taiyetos) and the cliffs of Outer Mani, and down on to the red roofs, esplanade and palm trees of the town itself. Koróni and Methóni, known in the Middle Ages as 'the Eyes of Venice', guarded the sea routes to Venice's eastern colonies. To the south, you can see Koróni's 1km sweep of sandy beach.

The ramparts surround houses, gardens, and a cemetery and monastery among pines and olives.
500m from the esplanade. Unenclosed.

METHÓNI

A fortified city from a historical romance, Methóni occupies a headland jutting into a vast bay sheltered by the island of

Sapiéntza, protected to landward by impregnable walls and a deep moat. Within, a 750m cobbled road leads from the inner keep past ruined mosques and churches, cracked spires and toppling arches to the octagonal Bourtzi tower on an island connected by a causeway. The Lion of St Mark, symbol of Venice, is emblazoned on the stonework to the left of the main gate, close to the sea. Sunset over the Bourtzi is best viewed from the long sandy beach east of the castle.

Modern Methóni, outside the walls, is a lively tourist resort in summer, reverting to a somnolent farming and fishing town out of season.

63km southwest of Kalamata. Castle, overlooking Methóni harbour (tel: 0731 25363). Open: daily, except Monday, 8.30am–3pm. Admission charge.

Rusting Venetian cannon adorn the battlements overlooking the tranquil harbour at Methóni

PÍLOS

The peaceful town of white- and cream-painted 19th-century houses overlooking the lagoon-like bay of Navarino is built around a small harbour (slated for development as a marina), guarded by the huge Neo Kastro.

51km west of Kalamata.

Neo Kastro (New Castle)

The castle was built by the Turks in the late 16th century to control the bay of Navarino and counter the Venetian forts at Methóni and Koróni. Recently restored, it contains a small museum with a fine, colourful collection of prints and lithographs of fantastically-costumed heroes of the War of Independence. The etching *Lendemain de Navarin* (*The Day After Navarino*) shows a disconsolate Turk clinging to a spar among the wreckage of his fleet.

Above Pílos, 500m from the harbour. Open: daily, 8.30am–3pm. Admission charge.

NAVARINO

The calm bay sheltered by the islands of Navarino and Sfaktiria attracted seafarers to Pílos from King Nestor, the elder statesman of the *Iliad* and the *Odyssey*, Homer's epics of the Trojan War, to Venetian and Turkish fleets in medieval and modern times.

On 20 October 1827, a Turkish fleet anchored in the bay was sunk by a flotilla of British, French and Russian ships commanded by the British Admiral Lord Codrington. Codrington's instructions were to observe, but when the Turks fired on one of the allied ships they responded in kind. The sinking of the Turkish fleet helped to decide the War of Independence in favour of the Greeks.

Precarious wooden balconies overhang
Andhritsaina's streets

THE CENTRAL PELOPONNESE

The heartland of the Peloponnese is a
blend of rugged mountains, rolling hills
and farming valleys filled with olive trees.

ANDRÍTSAINA (ANDHRITSAINA)

A charming, old-fashioned hill town
surrounded by barren peaks,
Andhritsaina rises from a main square
dominated by an enormous plane tree,
and in summer is full of café tables.
Many of its older houses have tiled roofs
and overhanging second storeys.
65km from Tripolis.

KARÍTAINA

Commanding the Alfiós valley, the 13th-
century baronial castle of the Frankish de
Bruyères family balances precariously
above the half-deserted medieval village.
Halfway up the steep path to the citadel
stands a marble bust, erected in 1939, of
Theodoros Kolokotronis, the great
general whose forces garrisoned the
castle in the 1821–30 War of
Independence.
55km from Tripolis. Unenclosed.

MANTINEIA

Founded in about 500BC, Mantineia was
destroyed by the Spartans in 385BC and
rebuilt in 371BC when Thebes was
victorious over Sparta. The ruins date
from the 371 rebuilding, and of
particular interest are the massive town
walls, over 4m thick and almost 4km in
length, with 10 gates and 120 towers.
*Unenclosed. 11km north of Tripolis on the
main road to Olympia.*

MEGALÓPOLIS (MAGALOPOLI)

Relics of the ancient city, built between
371 and 368BC by Epaminondas of
Thebes to curb the power of Sparta,
include the foundations of the 66m by
53m assembly hall and the lower rows of
a 59-tier theatre which seated nearly
20,000.
*1km north of the modern town of
Magalopoli on the Karitaina road.
Signposted. Open: daily, except Monday,
8.30am–3pm. Admission free.*

TRIPOLIS

The quiet market town of Tripolis is the
hub of the Peloponnese road and rail
networks, and the gateway to the more
exciting southern Peloponnese. Tripolis
stands amid farmland on a 600m plateau
ringed by mountains. Destroyed by the
Turkish general Ibrahim Pasha during
the War of Independence, it is a far cry
from the holiday hotspots and a good

place to come if you want to see everyday Greek life unaffected by the tourism business.

180km southwest of Athens.

VASSAI

The dramatically sited Temple of Apollo Epikourios (Apollo the Succourer) at Vassai stands 1,128m above sea level, looking out over the blue slopes of the Arkadian mountain ranges. The temple's tottering pillars are braced by a web of scaffolding and it is protected from the elements by a vast high-tech marquee. Built in 450–420BC, it is one of the best preserved of the ancient temples and is attributed to Iktinos, one of the builders of the Parthenon. It was rediscovered, almost intact, by the French architect and archaeologist Joachim Bocher in 1765. Like those of the Parthenon, its friezes were acquired by the British Museum in the early 19th century and are still exhibited in London.

With 15 Doric columns on its long sides and six on each end, the temple is much narrower than is common and, unusually, is oriented north to south instead of east to west.

65km southeast from Olympia. Signposted.
Unenclosed.

The main square in Andhritsaina where a large plane tree provides shelter from the sun

THE FRANKS OF THE MOREA

In 1204 the Frankish soldiers of the Fourth Crusade turned on the Byzantine Empire, sacked Constantinople, and carved the empire (of which Greece was then part) into a federation of Latin kingdoms. One of these knights, Geoffrey de Villehardouin, took the Peloponnese, then called Achaia or the Morea, dividing it into 12 baronies which he gave to his followers. The Frankish barons occupied and added to Byzantine castles such as Acrocorinth and Monemvasía, or built new ones like Karitaina and Mistra. The Latin mini-states in Greece lasted just half a century before being driven out by a newly assertive Byzantium. In 1259 William de Villehardouin was among the Frankish knights defeated and captured at Pelagonia in northern Greece by the exiled Byzantine Emperor, Michael VIII Paleologos. He was forced to surrender his three strongest castles, Monemvasia, Mystra and Great Maina. Two years later, the Byzantines reconquered Constantinople and gradually drove the Franks from their remaining strongholds.

The seven Doric columns of the Temple of Apollo are all that remain standing of Ancient Corinth

CORINTH AND AROUND

ARKHEA KÓRINTHOS
(Ancient Corinth)

Corinth's varying fortunes through the ages are reflected in the ruins of the ancient city, which span 800 years, from the 5th century BC to the 3rd century AD. A great power in the 8th century BC, Corinth was later overshadowed by Athens until again ascendant as chief of the League of Corinth under the Macedonian kings. In Roman times the city was one of the great imperial cities, but the fall of Rome, barbarian invasions and Turkish conquest eventually obliterated it. Ancient Corinth is actually situated at the foot of the hill of Akrokórinthos (Acrocorinth), 7km southwest of the modern city.

Highlights of the site are the Temple of Apollo, with seven of its 38 Doric columns intact, dating from the 6th century BC, and the Peirene Fountain with its stone arches and colonnade. Other relics include the 150m by 90m site of the Agorá and the foundations of the enormous *stoa* which occupied its south side. The seats of a small Roman *odeon*, carved from the rock in the 1st century AD, are clearly visible next to the much larger 18,000-seat theatre built in the 5th century BC and enlarged in the 3rd century BC by the Romans, who used it for gladiatorial contests.

The museum features Roman mosaics and statues, pottery and several small bronzes.

Ancient Corinth is 7km southwest of modern Corinth, signposted. Mousio Arkheologikou (Archaeological Museum) (tel: 0741 31207). Open: Monday, 11am–6pm; Tuesday to Sunday, 8am–6pm. Archaeological site (tel: 0741 31207). Open: daily, except Monday, 8am–6pm. Admission charge includes both.

AKROKÓRINTHOS
(Acrocorinth)
Towering on its 500m crag above the site of ancient Corinth, the immense ramparts of this medieval stronghold embrace Ancient Greek, Roman, Frankish and Turkish remnants. A Byzantine fortress, it was taken by the Franks in 1211 and added to by Frankish princes over the next 180 years. It passed back to Byzantium in 1394 and was later held by the Knights of St John, the Venetians and the Turks. The 15th-century ramparts, 3km long, are pierced by three gates, and inside there are two more walls built by the Byzantines. Within the walls are a dilapidated mosque and minaret, and a small church among the tumbled walls of the Turkish town. Beside the minaret is an ancient well, still providing water.

From the highest point, marked by a Corinthian capital atop a concrete pillar, there are awe-inspiring 360-degree views.
Acrocorinth Archaeological Site (tel: 0741 31207). Two kilometres above the archaeological site of ancient Corinth. Open: daily, except Monday, 8.30am–6pm. Admission charge.

DIÓRIGA KORÍNTHOU
(Corinth Canal)
The Corinth Canal, begun by a French company in 1882 and completed by the Greeks 11 years later, is today more a landmark than a shipping route. The canal helped make Piraeus Greece's major port, but it is too narrow for modern vessels and is used only by smaller cruise ships. It is 6.34km long, 23m wide and 80m below the land surface, and crossed by two bridges, the eastern one carrying the Athens-Patras National Road.

Several rulers of the region in ancient times (the Roman Emperor Nero among them) attempted to build a canal across the isthmus, though none succeeded. The Greek allies built a wall across the isthmus in 480BC to keep the Persians out, which remained in place until Venetian times. The Venetians and the Turks found it a useful source of stone and no sign of it survives.
On the main Patras-Athens highway.

KÓRINTHOS (Corinth)
Modern Corinth, repeatedly levelled by earthquakes (the most recent in 1981) is a modern seaside town which can be bypassed en route to the ancient site. There is little of interest here, though the town has plenty of shops and a few restaurants.

The Corinth Canal, 23m wide and 6km long

Market day at Areópolis

DEEP MÁNI

Deep Máni, a mountainous finger of land protected by cliffs and easily defended narrow passes, was never fully under Turkish control. The Maniot clans were virtually self-governing and spent their time feuding with each other from their tiny square castles when not allied in rebellion against Turkey. Feuds went on not only from village to village but between families in the same village, and rivals strove to build the tallest towers.

AREÓPOLIS

Once resounding to the shouts and gunfire of the Mavromichalis clan, this now quiet village is where the War of Independence against Turkish occupation began.
26km west of Yíthion.

KELEFÁ

The huge, empty grey shell of Kelefá Castle, built in the 17th century by the Turks to control the turbulent clans, guards the gateway to Deep Máni. To the north the village of Itilon stands beneath the grim peaks called the Pendadaktylos (the five-fingered).
4km northwest from Areópolis-Yíthion road on a rough track (signposted). Unenclosed.

KITA

Once the largest and most powerful of the towered villages, Kita looks from a distance like a miniature city of skyscrapers, but most of its towers have fallen into picturesque disrepair.
16km south of Areopolis.

KÓTRONAS

Ringed by steep rocky slopes, this out-of-the-way harbour village with a small stretch of east-facing pebbly beach sits at the end of a fjord-like bay.
40km south of Yíthion.

PASSAVA

The battlements of the 13th-century Frankish castle, now in ruins, can be seen from the Yíthion-Areópolis road only with difficulty (see Inner Máni and Ákra Taínaron tour, pages 80–1).
11km south of Yíthion.

PÓRTO KÁYIO (Porto Kaigio)

The tarred road ends here, at one of the

WAR OF INDEPENDENCE

Areópolis, gateway to the Deep Máni, was renamed after Ares, the war god, to honour its role as the starting place for the War of Independence (1821–30). The belligerent Maniots exploded out of their mountain eyries to join the *klephts* (Robin Hood-like brigands) and the pirate captains of the Aegean in revolt. They were aided by 'Philhellenes', foreign volunteers determined to free Greece from the Turkish yoke and restore its golden age. Turkey was crippled by the destruction of its fleet at Navarino and in 1829 Britain, Russia and France brokered a treaty creating a Greek homeland in the Peloponnese, Athens and Attica, the Sterea Ellas and a handful of Aegean islands, but leaving the rest of Greece in Turkish hands.

prettiest unspoiled bays in Greece. Once famous for its game birds – its name means 'Port of Quails' – it is still a favourite with locals during the autumn hunting season. *65km south of Yíthion.*

SPILAION DHIROÚ/DHIROU SPILIES (Dhirou Caves)

A 1.2km river flows through the Vlychadha Cavern, a wonderland of spires, cones, needles and stalactites. The tour by boat takes 30 minutes. The museum displays neolithic finds from the Alepotripa cave, still being explored. *7km west from the Areópolis-Yerolimín main road, signposted from Pirgos Dhirou (tel: 0733 52222). Open: June to September, daily, 8am–6pm; rest of the year, 8am–3pm. Admission charge. Museum open: daily, 8.30am–3pm. Separate admission charge.*

TAÍNARON

South of Porto Kaigio the potholed road runs through rugged, semi-desert scenery to end abruptly above the site of the 5th-century BC Temple of Poseidon, in a cave said to be one of the entrances to Hades, the land of the dead. The cave, little more than a depression in the rock, now houses donkeys and nothing remains of the temple. To the right, past a tiny pebble cove, the rough path passes the remains of a circular mosaic floor, exposed to the elements. Follow the path southwest over the headland to the Taínaron lighthouse and the southern tip of Greece, where cliffs plunge to dazzling azure water. *7km south of Pórto Káyio.*

VÁTHIA

Still ruinous but making a comeback thanks to tourism, the spectacular tower village of Váthia, atop a cactus-covered hill, is the best preserved of the Mani tower villages. Surrounded by bare hillsides, it is full of old houses and medieval bastions and keeps. *9km southeast from the port of Yerolimín.*

The river journey through the Dhirou caverns

The island fortress at Monemvasía, the Gibraltar of Greece

THE EAST COAST

ÁKRA MALÉA (Cape Malea)

Easternmost of the peninsulas of the southern Peloponnnese, mountainous Ákra Maléa (Cape Malea) points towards the island of Kíthira on the southern horizon. The cape's eastern side is rocky and inaccessible, and the main road ends about 11km south of Monemvasía.

KIPARISSIA

The white villas and cottages of Kiparissia stand among the cypress trees which give it its name, above a sweep of pebbly beach. The imposing slopes of the Párnon massif rise almost vertically behind the village.
40km north of Monemuasia.

LEONÍDHION

Precarious balconies overhang the streets of this pleasantly unchanged small town at the foot of a dizzyingly steep canyon running far into the mountains. Leonídhion stands 3km inland from its harbour and beach, the former a favourite with yacht sailors and the latter a magnet for holidaying Athenians.

Between the pebbly, 1km-long beach and the town is a delta of fertile farmland dotted with fruit trees, olive groves and colourful plantations of peppers, aubergines and tomatoes.
68km south of Navplion.

MONEMVASÍA

The dizzying 300m-high rock of Monemvasía, 400m offshore, is a natural fortress, added to by Byzantine, Frankish, Venetian and Turkish builders. It gives its name to malmsey wine, exported from the Aegean islands to Europe by the Venetians.

The name means 'one entrance', and with its cliffs and ramparts Monemvasía looks like a tough proposition for any belligerent besieger. In fact, it was frequently conquered when the defenders ran out of water. Populous until the early 19th century, it was taken and sacked by the Greeks during the War of Independence and the last permanent resident of the cragtop fortress died in 1906.

The settlement on the rock and on the mainland opposite falls into three parts: the kastro, Pano Kastro and Yefira.
100km southeast of Sparta.

Kastro (Castle)

The lower town, within the medieval walls, is a maze of arches, alleys, steps and tall 15th-century Venetian houses, many of them restored as hotels or holiday apartments. Strict rules ensure that houses are rebuilt in traditional style, and no vehicles can pass the iron-bound gates through the medieval walls. Even in high summer you can wander through cobbled lanes lined with crumbling walls and wild fig trees without meeting another soul, though in its medieval heyday it had a population of 30,000 and as many as 40 churches.

Pano Kastro (Upper Castle)

The early medieval town on the flat top of the crag is a honeycomb of shattered walls and collapsed archways. The only intact building is the late 13th-century church of Ayia Sofia, with some interesting frescos.

Yefira (Bridge)

The modern fishing and tourism town on the mainland takes its name from the causeway and bridge which connect it with the castle. Restaurants and cafés surround the harbour and there is a pebbly beach to the north. There is a sandier beach, with fine views of the castle rock, at Pori, 3km north of Yefira on the main road.

PARALIA ASTROS

The shell of a Frankish castle on a headland overlooks a yacht and fishing harbour at the north end of a 2km crescent of sandy, pebbly beach. Behind the village, a mixture of 18th- and 19th-century stone houses below the castle and modern villas around the harbour, a sea of olives laps at the foothills of Parnon, 2km inland. Inland lies an immense freshwater lagoon ringed with reeds, a magnet for kingfishers, swans and wading birds.
30km south of Návplion.

Kastro (Castle)

The 15th-century castle at Paralia Astros has outstanding panoramic views down the east coast, across the Argolikos Kólpos (Argolic Gulf) and the island of Spétsai (Spetses), and north to Návplion.
On the hill above the town. Unenclosed.

The Venetian bell-tower within the lower Kastro at Monemvasía

THE EVROTAS VALLEY

MISTRÁS (Mistra)

The ultimate medieval fairy-tale castle, with a complex of ruined domes, palaces and ramparts surrounding a pinnacle on the east flank of Taiyetos, above modern Sparta. Fortified by the Villehardouin princes to seal the pass above it, Mistra passed into Byzantine hands after the battle of Pelagonia (1259) and held out against the Turks until 1460, seven years after the fall of Constantinople. It was repeatedly besieged during the struggles for control of the Peloponnese in the 16th and 17th centuries, and during the War of Independence, when it was finally

Medieval Mistra

burned and abandoned.

The site is crowned by a fortress on a crag, with steps and paths winding through the ruined buildings below, several of which are being restored. The most important buildings are the frescoed church of Ayia Sofia, immediately below the castle; the imposing four-storey Palace of the Despots; and Perivleptos, Panayia and Ayios Nikolaos churches. Near the main gate, a small museum exhibits a collection of column pedestals and fragments.

6km from Sparta, the lower Main Gate is 1km from the modern village of Mistras. The upper Fortress Gate is 2km further uphill (tel: 0731 93377). Signposted. Open: daily, except Monday, 8am–6pm. Admission charge.

SPÁRTI (Sparta)

Founded in 1836 by settlers made homeless by the destruction of Mistra in the War of Independence, modern Sparta shows little connection with the city-state which dominated the entire region from the 6th to the 4th century BC. Ancient Sparta depended for defence on the legendary courage and prowess of its warriors, not on fortifications, and, unlike their Athenian rivals, the Spartans built no great stone temples, monuments or public buildings. Modern Sparta is a pleasant enough market town set in breathtaking scenery, with the jagged, lunar summits of Taiyetos jostling for space on its western skyline.
60km south of Tripoli.

Arkheologiko Mousio (Archaeological Museum)

Housed in an elegant neo-classical building in a statue-filled garden shaded by tall palms, the collection includes mosaics, marble reliefs from the 6th century BC, a bust of a Spartan warrior from 490–480BC, a colossal Hellenistic head of Hercules, and a collection of scowling votive masks from the nearby Sanctuary of Artemis Orthia.
East side of Leoforos K. Palaeoglou, between Evangelistrias and Lykourgos (tel: 0731 25363). Open: daily, except Monday, 8.30am–3pm. Admission charge.

YERÁKI

The dramatic ruined fortress of Yeráki on its hilltop is visible far away across the

The hilltop castle at Mistra, the last outpost of the Byzantine Empire

flat bottom of the Evrotas valley, above the modern village of the same name. There is an awesome view of the saw-toothed Taiyetos, 20km west. The shattered shells of several small churches surround the castle walls.

4km east of Yeráki village, 1km from main road. Unenclosed.

YÍTHION

Close to the mouth of the wide, fertile Evrotas flood plain, Yíthion dozes by a mirror-calm harbour sheltered by Kranai, the island where Paris and Helen spent their first night of passion together before fleeing to Troy. Elegant old mansions with wrought-iron balconies mount in tiers above the port, relics of its 19th-century heyday when its fleet of schooners carried all the trade of the region.

48km south of Sparta.

Mousio Tzannetakis (Tzannetakis Museum)

This is a small museum situated in an 18th-century tower, devoted to the history of the Mani. Exhibits include books, writings and paintings.

On the island of Kranai, reached by a causeway from the harbour esplanade (tel: 0733 22676/24631). Open: daily, 9am–1pm and 5pm-9pm. Admission charge.

Arkaiou Theatrou (Ancient Theatre)

Built by the Romans in the 1st century AD, the compact theatre has 13 tiers of seats.

East end of Odhos Arkaiou Theatrou. Unenclosed.

Mansions built by wealthy 19th-century shipowners line the harbour at Yíthion

ITHOMI, KALÁMAI (KALAMATA) AND THE OUTER MANI

ITHOMI (Ancient Messini/Messene)

A row of grim grey towers on a spur of Ithomi Oros (Mount Ithomi), remnant of a 10km ring of ramparts, guards the ruins of Ancient Messini, an agorá, theatre and stadium built in the 4th century BC. Messíni, destroyed after rebelling against Sparta, was rebuilt by the Theban ruler Epaminondas after his defeat of Sparta at Leuktra in 379BC. There is a fine aerial view of the site from the village of Mavromati, 300m above it. From the Lakonian Gate, 1.5km uphill from Mavromati, there is a panoramic view over the pastoral patchwork of the Messinian plain.

11km from modern Messíni, and confusingly signposted Ancient Messini, Ithomi, Archaic Ithomi, Ancient Messini and Ithomi Archaeological Site. Unenclosed.

KALÁMAI (Kalamata)

The largest town in the southern Peloponnese with 40,000 inhabitants, Kalamata is of little interest to sightseers.

EARTHQUAKES

Southern Greece has been struck by earthquakes throughout history, which accounts for the ruinous state of many of the ancient temples. Kalámai (Kalamata) has been particularly unlucky, being rocked by quake after quake over the last two centuries. In September 1986 it was hit again. Much of the damage has been repaired with aid from the European Community, but the town still has a shell-shocked air.

The town was completely destroyed in the War of Independence and since then has been rocked by earthquakes several times, most recently in 1986.

KARDHAMÍLI

This little town of sturdy 18th- and 19th-century balconied houses with its 2km beach of white pebbles and miniature harbour overlooking the Messiniakos Kólpos (Messinian Gulf) is the gateway to the Mani, a mountainous land of vendettas whose noble families built themselves miniature castles from which to defy their rivals. One of these quaint square towers, the stronghold of the Mourtzinos family, can be seen at the ghost village of Palaeo Kardhamíli (Old Kardhamíli) near by. It was built in 1808. Next to it stands a Byzantine church with an unusual stone spire decorated with a carved floral pattern.

30km southeast of Kalamata.
Palaeo Kardhamíli is 750m from the west end of Kardhamíli, signposted Old Kardamíli.

STOUPA

A delightful, relaxed resort on a sheltered bay with a sandy crescent of west-facing beach, with Ákra Akritas on the horizon, backed by a dramatic landscape – the sheer, treeless and almost uninhabited slopes of the Taïyetos range.

35km southeast of Kalamata.

THALAMES

The square-built stone houses and antique pantiled Byzantine church of Thalames perch on a steep limestone hillside among olive groves and cypresses. Below it the slopes plunge away to pebbly coves and hidden beaches.

50km southeast of Kalamata.

Mousio Máni (Máni Museum)

This gloriously eclectic and eccentric collection of tools, weapons, furniture, banknotes, coins, books, portraits and posters should not be missed. The ground floor houses cases of potsherds, glassware and rusting swords and muskets while the upper floor is decorated with naive posters depicting Greece's struggles for independence. *On main street of the village, signposted (tel: 0721 74414). Open: daily, 8am–8pm; closed October to April. Admission charge.*

TAÏYETOS ÓROS (Mount Taïyetos)

Mount Taïyetos forms the jagged backbone of the southern Peloponnese, running from the centre of the province to form the peninsula of Ákra Taínaron. The western slopes of the massif are barren, but its eastern flanks, overlooking the Evrotas plain, are cloaked in fir and pine. Atop its highest peak, once sacred to Apollo, stands the shrine of Profitis Ilias (Prophet Elijah), the scene of a colourful annual festival (18–20 July, see Festivals). The ascent to the 2,407m peak can only be made on foot and should be attempted only by fit, experienced mountain walkers. The summits of the range are snow-capped as late as June.

Nine-kilometre long stone walls once surrounded the ancient city of Messini, protecting it from rival Sparta

THE NORTH COAST AND ACHAIA

ACHAIA CLAUSS
A charming mock-Bavarian castle in the hills is the headquarters of Greece's oldest winery. Founded in 1861 by Gustav Clauss (1825–1908), Achaia Clauss makes red and white table wines and dessert wines, all of which can be sampled and bought.
5km from the centre of Patras, signposted (tel: 8075 312). Open: daily, 9am–7.30pm. Admission free.

CHLEMOÚTSI (Castle Tornese)
Round bastions and sheer walls surround the vaulted inner hall and courtyard of this hilltop stronghold. Built in 1220, it was the seat of Geoffrey II Villehardouin's princedom of Achaia, as this region is still called. From the ramparts, you can see the islands of Zákinthos and Kefallinia.
86km southwest of Patras, 4km from Kilini. Open: daily, except Monday, 8.30am–5pm. Admission charge.

KALÁVRITA
This leafy mountain village has a special significance for Greeks. Near here, in 1821, Archbishop Germanos called for the beginning of the War of Independence. Many of the inhabitants were martyred by the Germans in 1943 on suspicion of harbouring resistance fighters. Kalávrita's main attraction is the narrow-gauge railway running through a deep canyon to Diakofto, on the Gulf of Corinth (see The Dhiakoptón to Kalávrita Railway tour, pages 82–3).

KILLÍNI (Kilini)
A fishing harbour on the tip of a west-pointing headland, Kilini offers a long sandy beach and the opportunity of a day trip to Zákinthos.

OLIMBÍA (Olympia)
The peaceful modern village of 900 people exists only to service visitors to ancient Olympia, the site of the Olympic Games for over 1,000 years. Most of the buildings on the archaeological site have been reduced to their foundations, but it is easy to picture the stadium packed with cheering crowds.

Altis (Sanctuary)
The heart of Olympia and sacred to Zeus, the Sanctuary covered an area of 200 sq m. The Doric Temple of Zeus, its most important structure, was demolished in the 6th century AD by an earthquake, though its massive remains are still imposing. It was this temple that contained the huge statue of Zeus that was one of the Seven Wonders of the World. Some columns of the neighbouring Temple of Hera have been rebuilt.

Column bases of the Palestra at Olympia, training ground for the competitors

Ergasteirion (Workshop of Phidias)

Built for Phidias, the greatest sculptor of classical times, who worked on his statue of Zeus here. In Byzantine times it became a church.

Leonidhion

Donated in the 4th century BC by Leonidas of Naxos, the Leonidhion was a luxurious inn for the rulers and dignitaries who visited the games. The Romans added a central pool to its four wings of rooms around a courtyard.

Mousio (Museum)

The most striking exhibits are the helmet of Miltiades, the victor of Marathón, found buried beneath the stadium as an offering to Zeus; the superb friezes from the Temple of Zeus, representing the legendary battle between the Lapiths and Centaurs; the statue of Hermes of about 350BC, discovered in 1877; and statues of Roman emperors.

Palestra

A Hellenistic double colonnade surrounded this training arena, where wrestlers and other athletes sparred.

Stadion (Stadium)

The grassy stadium with its 193m course seated 20,000 spectators. No women were admitted, except the priestess of Demeter, on pain of death.

Archaeological Site (tel: 0624 22517), 2km from modern Olympia, clearly signposted. Open: Monday to Saturday, 7.30am–5pm; Sunday, 8am–5pm.
Museum (tel: 0624 22529), opposite archaeological site. Open: Monday, 11am–5pm; Tuesday to Friday, 8am–5pm; weekends and holidays, 8am–3pm. Admission charge: includes site and museum.

PÁTRAI (Patras)

Greece's third largest city is the gateway to Greece for those arriving by sea from Italy. It was rebuilt after being virtually destroyed in World War II. The café-filled squares and avenues of the town centre are overlooked by a crumbling, 1,000-year-old castle.
212km west of Athens.

The cathedral of Ayios Andreas (St Andrew) in Patras

Ayios Andreas

The largest church in Greece, built in 1979 to house the gold casket containing the head of the saint, who was executed by the Romans in Patras, and which was returned to Patras from St Peter's by Pope Paul VI in 1964.
Platia Ayiou Andreou. Open: daily, except during services. Admission free.

Kastro (Castle)

The battlements of a 9th-century Byzantine castle with Frankish, Venetian and Turkish additions rise from the peak of a wooded hill close to the city centre.
Southeast end of Odhos Ayios, Nikolaou. Unenclosed.

Inner Máni and Ákra Taínaron

The Máni is dotted with castles, Byzantine churches and ruined towers. The 136km route follows newly built roads and is well signposted. *Allow 8 hours.*

Leave Yíthion by the coast road towards Areópolis, passing the long beach of Mavrovoúni and then winding through wooded hills.

1 PASSAVA

The hilltop battlements of the 13th-century Frankish castle are

hard to spot from the road. Look out for the signpost to Khosiario (Xosiario), 9km after leaving Yíthion. Park at the Country Tavern (signposted in English) and pick your way up a very rough track. Only the walls still stand. Allow 1 hour.

A narrow pass ends in a fertile plain below the village of Vakhós (Vahos) and the bare flanks of Kouskouni.

2 KELEFÁ

Signposted to your right, 4km off the main road on a rough track (park by the village cemetery and walk the last 1km), Kelefá's mighty walls sheltered a strong Turkish garrison.

After 1km the main road emerges high above the west coast of the Máni, with the Messinian peninsula to the west.

3 AREÓPOLIS

The 'capital of the Máni' is ringed with tumbledown houses and fallen walls, but many old mansions are being restored as second homes.

The road south balances between desert mountains and sea cliffs on a fertile strip of olive groves and grainfields divided by dry-

stone walls. At Pirgos Dhirou turn right (signposted Spilaia Dhirou/Caves) for 5km.

4 SPILAION DHIROÚ (THE DHIROU CAVES)

Allow 25 minutes for the tour of the Vlychadha Cavern and underground river (see page 71).

The main road bypasses a chain of half-ruined tower villages like clusters of miniature skyscrapers. At the hamlet of Ayios Yioryios look seaward for your first view of Tigáni. Turn right to Stavríon, a 4km detour, and park at the tiny collection of towers 1km beyond. A donkey track leads downhill to Tigáni. The walk is strenuous and involves picking your way among jagged boulders. Allow 1 hour.

5 TIGÁNI

The clifftop castle gets its name, which means 'frying pan', from the rocky peninsula it stands on. The handle of the frying pan is a natural causeway, making it a superb natural stronghold.

Return to the main coast road and turn right.

6 TOURLOTÍ

To the left, 1.5km north of Kita and 300m above the new road, the 9th-century domed church of Tourlotí is one of the prettiest of dozens of Byzantine churches in the Máni.

7 KITA

The largest tower village, Kita was the seat of the Máni's most powerful clans. Tourism has brought some life back to the half-ruined village.

The sea is hidden by the Kavo Grosso plateau. After 5km the road descends to the

half-abandoned harbour of Yerolimin, then winds through hills, passing through Alika.

8 VÁTHIA

The towers of Váthia house a Greek National Tourist Organisation guesthouse (see page 177). A tiny pebbly beach 1km below offers swimming.
Continue towards the cape.

9 PÓRTO KÁYIO AND ÁKRA TAÍNARON

The lovely lagoon is overlooked by a tiny Turkish fort and is a favourite yacht anchorage.

Ákra Taínaron is 5km south and you must walk the final kilometre to Greece's southern tip (see page 71).

Backtrack to Alika and turn right, cresting a pass 3km above Tsíkkaliá (Tsikalia). There are sweeping views of the Lakonikós Kólpos (Laconic Gulf) and Ákra Malea before the road plunges 300m to the sea at Kokkala and its pebbly white beach. It then follows the contours of the coast up to Kótronas and turns inland to Areópolis.

The barren peninsula of Tigáni is ringed by the ramparts of a Byzantine castle

The Dhiakoptón (Dhiakofton) to Kalávrita Railway

The narrow-gauge rack-and-pinion railway between Dhiakoptón, on the shores of the Gulf of Corinth, and Kalávrita offers the most spectacular train ride in Greece, passing through a series of tunnels in a narrow mountain gorge.

Originally drawn by tiny steam engines – one still stands at each of the two stations – the train is now driven by sturdy little French-built diesel locomotives which pull two carriages seating 68 people. First- and second-class seating is available. Six departures daily each way; no reservations needed.

The 23km journey takes 68 minutes each way. Allow 3 hours (4 if visiting the Mega Spileon monastery).

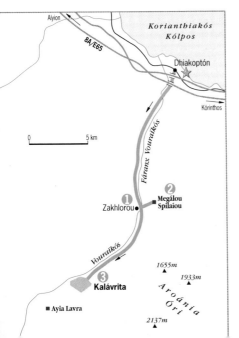

Leaving Dhiakoptón the train rattles through lemon groves, passes under the busy National Road and enters the steep-sided Vouraïkós gorge.

Towering grey and pink limestone crags and sheer cliffs pocked with caves and holes loom above the track as the train climbs laboriously through pine woods. As the going gets steeper the rack-and-pinion gear is engaged and the train weaves in and out of a series of gallery tunnels, moving at little more than walking speed.

1 ZAKHLOROU (ZAHLOROU)

After about 40 minutes the tiled roofs and white houses of Zakhlorou emerge from the chestnut and cherry trees. The train stops here briefly for passengers wishing to visit the monastery at Mega Spileon, which involves a steep, 45-minute walk.

2 MEGÁLOU SPILAÍOU (MEGA SPILEON)

Founded in the 8th century when its miraculous icon of the Virgin was revealed to two monks by a shepherd girl, the monastery was rebuilt this century after a fire and its exterior is dull. Inside, the icon is surrounded by gold gift-offerings, watches, chains and rings, and you can just make out the frescos painted on the sooty ceiling. The excellent small museum contains icons, holy relics and 18th- and 19th-century vestments, and is open daily, 8am–1pm and 5pm–sunset. Admission charge (small). Proper dress is necessary.

Above Zakhlorou the slope is not steep and the train rattles at speed towards Kalavrita, beneath cliffs sculpted by erosion.

3 KALÁVRITA

The small town stands at the head of a fertile valley, 750m above sea level and

Kalávrita station is the southern terminus of the Dhiakoptón railway

dominated by the saw-edged peaks of the Aroánia Óri (Aroania range). At the Monastery of Ayia Lavra, 7km from the town, Archbishop Germanos proclaimed the revolt on 25 March 1821 which became the War of Independence. The monastery, burned by the Turks in 1821 and the Germans in 1943, houses a small museum (open 8am–1pm and 5pm–sunset). The Koimisos tis Theotokou (Cathedral of the Virgin Mary) in Kalávrita's main square was also burned by both Turks and Germans. One of its two clocks is permanently stopped at 2.34pm, the time at which 1,436 villagers were massacred by the Nazis on 13 December 1943, an event also marked by a monument above the village. History aside, Kalávrita is a pleasant, quiet village with a cool *platia* shaded by trees in front of the cathedral.

Miniature locomotive on the Dhiakoptón railway line

Stereá Ellás

Stereá Ellás (Sterea Ellas) is a narrow coastal strip bounded in the south by the calm waters of the Korinthiakós Kólpos (Gulf of Corinth) and dominated in the north by a series of thinly-populated mountain ranges. From east to west, these are Panaitolikón, Vardhoúsia, Gióna and Parnassós. In the north-west the Amvrakikós Kólpos (Amvrakic Gulf) takes a bite out of the coast and separates the region from neighbouring Ipiros (Epirus).

The sightseeing high point is the ancient sanctuary of Delfí (Delphi), second only to the Acropolis among the classical sites of Greece. There are medieval castles aplenty, too. Inland, the region displays striking mountain scenery, including one of Greece's handful of ski resorts, while on the west coast the Ionian Sea laps at some of the mainland's least-visited beaches. A major highway from Athens and Thebes passes through Levádhia (Livadhia), Arákhova and Delphi before meeting the coast at Itéa and skirts the Gulf of Corinth on its way to Andírrion, Mesolóngion and points north and west.

Ossios Loukas monastery has some of the finest Byzantine frescos and mosaics in Greece

A gold mosaic decorates a doorway at Ossios Loukas monastery

STEREA ELLAS

Fársala

30

Néon Monastírion

Dhomokos

Almirós

Pagastikós Kólpos

Soúrpi

Argalastí   Skíathos

Plataniá

Alónnisos

Peristéra

Skópelos

1726m

Óthris

Dhíavlos Trikeri

Glífa

Istiaía

61m

Makrakómi

Lamia

3

1/E75

Kaména Voúrla

Loutrá Aidhipsoú

Vórtios Evvoikós Kólpos

Limni

Évvoia

Thermopílai

Arkítsa

0   20   40 km

2406m   2510m

Amfíklia

Kifissós

Atalánti

Malesína

1743m

Kími

Gkióna

3

Psakhná

Mórnos   48   Ámfissa

Lidhoríkion

Delphi

2457m

Parnassós

Khairónia

Kástron

Paralimní

Khalkís

Limni

E65

Galaxídhion

Itéa

Dhístomon

Arákhova

Ósios Loukás

48

Orkhomenós

Levádhia

Ilíki

Aliyérion

Eretria

44

ávpaktos

Nótios Evvoikós Kólpos

44

Thívai

Skála Oropoú

Aíyion

Korinthiakós Kólpos

Thísvi

Plataiaí

Erithraí

3

Párnis Óros

1413m

Marathón

Pórto Yermenón

Mandra

Elevsís

Kalávrita

8A/E65

Kiáton

Mégara

8A/E94

Rafína

Peloppónnisos

Kórinthos

Salamís

Piraiévs

ATHÍNAI

DELPHI ROAD

ARÁKHOVA

Though its steep-roofed, half-timbered houses tremble to the passing of heavy traffic on the main highway which runs through the town, Arákhova is quite peaceful. Off the busy main street, lined with restaurants and souvenir shops selling rugs and sheepskin coats, it is pleasantly peaceful and its location – above Delphi, commanding a pass over the shoulder of 2,457m Parnassós – affords fine views in all directions. With bare hills above and below, it has a cool, almost alpine climate and Athenians come here to ski on the Parnon pistes above the town as late as April.

34km west of Levádhia.

KHAIRÓNIA/CHAIRONEIA (Heronia)

A gigantic marble lion guards the battlefield where in 338BC the pikemen and cavalry of Macedon crushed the combined forces of the southern city-states, led by Thebes. The 5.5m statue marked the grave of the warriors of the élite Sacred Band of Thebes, who fought to the death. Greek guerrilla fighters in the War of Independence smashed it open, hoping to find treasure, but found nothing. It was pieced together some 80 years later and re-erected. The town is also the birthplace of Plutarch, the Greek historian and philosopher (*c.*46–*c.*120).

11km north of Levádhia.

Arákhova commands the pass over Parnassós

LEVÁDHIA

There is no sign today of the meadows from which this unkempt but not unappealing town takes its name. In medieval times Levádhia was the most important town in the region, thanks to its strategic site controlling routes between Athens and the west and north. Although a handful of the old Turkish-style houses with overhanging upper storeys and wrought-iron balconies survive, and the dome of a derelict mosque can be spotted at the corner of Tsogka and Stratigo Ioannou, for the most part Levádhia is uncompromisingly modern.

A clear, fast-running stream springs from a source below the limestone crag on which the town's 14th-century castle stands, and is crossed near its source by a hump-backed Turkish mule bridge. It takes about 20 minutes to scramble through pine woods to the dilapidated castle, but the climb is worth it for the view of Parnassós to the west and the fertile farmlands of the eastern plain.
190km west of Athens.
Frourio (Fortress), 750m from town centre, signposted. Unenclosed.

ORKHOMENÓS

Just outside the unassuming agricultural town of Orkhomenós are the ruins of the ancient settlement, a powerful city in Mycenaean times. The most prominent remnants are the theatre and, next to it, a collapsed Mycenaean chamber-tomb dating from the city's heyday in the 14th century BC. Climb to the top of the hill on which the acropolis of the city once stood for an extensive bird's-eye view of the ancient site.
11km northeast of Levadhia; 1km east of the town centre on the road to Kástron.
Open: daily, except Monday, 8.30am–3pm.

ÓSIOS LOUKÁS

The Byzantine church was completed in 1019 on the site of an earlier hermitage of St Luke the Styriote, who was celebrated for his miraculous healings and prophecies. It is built in the formal style, with a central dome over an eight-sided body. The best-preserved of the great Byzantine churches, it has 16 arched windows surrounded by mosaics of the prophets and surmounted by angels. The apse is dominated by a mosaic of the Virgin and Child. The exterior is a typical patchwork of brick and stone in the Byzantine manner.

Next to the main church is the Church of the Theotokos, where services are still held. On the gallery of the second floor of the monastic buildings opposite, note the wooden bar and metal chimes which are struck to call the monastery's handful of monks to prayer.
9km south of the main Levádhia/Itéa road, follow signs to Dhístomon, then to Ósios Loukás (tel: 3213571). Open: daily, except Monday, 8.30am–3pm. Admission charge.

The monastic church of Ossios Loukas is the best-preserved of Greece's Byzantine churches

Delfi

(Delphi)

*T*he centre of the Ancient Greek world, the Delphi site is the most powerfully magnetic classical site outside Athens. Much of its charisma stems from its location, carefully chosen by its founders to amplify the awed emotions of pilgrims as they approached the sanctuaries and the oracle.

Close to the mouth of a deep gorge in the side of Parnassós, Delphi is ringed by massive peaks and looks south over a delta of olive groves which flows from the foothills down to the shores of the Gulf of Corinth. The amphitheatrical plan of the Sanctuary of Apollo is echoed by the 300m cliffs which loom above it.
The archaeological sites are separated by the main Delphi-Arákhova road.

Ieros Dhromos (the Sacred Way and the main site)

The most fully restored buildings of the main site are the porticoed Treasury of

The treasury of the Athenians at Delphi

THE ORACLE OF DELPHI

The earth-mother Gaia was worshipped at Delphi from the 14th century BC through priestesses who were intoxicated by fumes rising from fissures in the earth. With the advent of the Dorians, Gaia was supplanted by Apollo and the site became his greatest sanctuary. Apollo's mouthpiece was the Sybil or Pythia, whose tranced utterings in answer to pilgrims' questions were translated into verse by her priests. The answers, ambiguous as they were, were not forecasts but advice.

the Athenians; the votive offering of the
Athenians, a Doric building erected in
490–480BC to commemorate the victory of
Marathón; the 4th-century BC Temple of
Apollo with six of its 50-plus Doric
columns standing; the 2nd-century BC
Theatre; and the 3rd-century BC Stadium.
Just above the Treasury of the Athenians a
very ordinary-looking boulder marks the
location of the famed Oracle.

These and the foundations of other
treasuries are connected by the Sacred
Way, a broad, stepped road which zig-zags
from the main entrance to the Stadium,
from which there are fine views of the site
and of the Temple of Athena, below the
main road.

*1km east of the modern village of Delphi,
above the Delphi-Arákhova road (tel: 0265
82313). Open: Monday to Friday,
7.30am–6pm; weekends and holidays,
8.30am–2.45pm. Admission charge.*

The 3rd-century BC stadium and the columns of
the Temple of Apollo at Delphi

Mousio Arkheologiko (Archaeological Museum)

One of the finest museums in Greece,
containing fragments of friezes, *kouroi*,
bronzes of griffons and sphinxes, ivory
figurines and heads of Artemis and Apollo,
and a splendid lifesize statue of a bull in
silver and gold. Top billing goes to the
Bronze Charioteer, the masterpiece of an
unknown artist of around 478BC. The site
was excavated by French archaeologists,
and most of the museum labelling is in
French and Greek.

*100m west of entrance to main archaeological
site, signposted (tel: 0265 82313). Open:
Monday, noon–6.15; Tuesday to Friday,
7.30am–6.15pm; weekends and public
holidays, 8.30am–2.15pm. Admission charge.*

Tholos (Rotunda)

Below the Sanctuary of Apollo stood two
temples of Athena, a 6th-century BC Doric
building which was abandoned in the 4th
century BC and replaced by a newer,
smaller temple. Only the foundations of
these remain. Between the sites of the
two temples stand the three surviving
columns of one of Delphi's most fully
reconstructed relics, the Tholos. This
circular 4th-century building was
probably a shrine to Gaia.

*500m east of main archaeological site, below
the Delphi-Arákhova road. Telephone,
opening hours and admission charge as for
main archaeological site.*

Vrisi Kastalias (Kastalian Spring)

The sacred spring, a mere trickle of water
for most of the year, emerges from a
narrow gorge between the two cliffs
which dominate the site of the Sanctuary.
Here, pilgrims washed themselves before
entering the Sanctuary. Two stone basins
used for this ritual can be seen carved in
the base of the cliff.

*100m east of the entrance to the Sanctuary
of Apollo. Closed for stabilisation of rocks.*

GODS AND HEROES OF

APHRODITE

Born from the sea, Aphrodite was the goddess of love and beauty. Her most important temple on the mainland was at Corinth.

APOLLO

Apollo was the god of male beauty and patron of the fine arts. His greatest sanctuary was at Delphi, but he was also worshipped at Corinth and Vassai (Vassae).

ARES

The god of war and lover of Aphrodite.

ARTEMIS

Twin sister of Apollo, Artemis the huntress is the goddess of chastity. Vravróna and Delphi were her most important temples.

Frieze depicting the marriage of Athena and Herakles

Zeus hurling a thunderbolt

ASKLEPIOS

The god of healing and son of Apollo. His major shrine was at Epídhavros.

ATHENA

The patron goddess of Athens had many aspects. She was the deity of wisdom, arts and crafts, and of victory. Her greatest temple was the Parthenon.

DEMETER

Goddess of fertility, worshipped principally at Elevsís.

DIONYSOS

The god of wine, joy and revelry, worshipped in Athens and on Mount Parnassós.

HADES

The king of the dead, whose oracle was the Nekromantion at Efira (Efyra).

ANCIENT GREECE

LETO

A minor goddess, lover of Zeus and mother of Apollo and Artemis.

PERSEPHONE

The daughter of Demeter and wife of Hades, Persephone was the goddess of death and renewal. Worshipped with her husband at the Nekromantion.

POSEIDON

The god of the sea, storms and earthquakes, second only to his brother Zeus, Poseidon's main shrines were at Athens and Cape Soúnion.

ZEUS

King of the gods and ruler of the world, Zeus was worshipped principally at Olympia and Dhodhóni (Dodoni).

HELIOS

The sun-god. Many of the tiny mountain chapels of Ayios Ilias (the prophet Elijah) may once have been his temples, an interesting play on the similarly-pronounced names.

HEPHAISTOS

God of fire and metal, hence of smiths, and husband of Aphrodite. Worshipped at his principal temple, now called the Thission, in Athens.

HERA

Hera was the wife of Zeus, greatest of the gods, and is the goddess of marriage. Her main temples were at Árgos and Olympia.

HERMES

The messenger of the gods, and so the god of commerce, communication and eloquence.

HESTIA

Hestia was the goddess of hearth and home.

Poseidon

The extensive Venetian harbour fortifications of Návpaktos

THE GULF OF CORINTH

ÁMFISSA

A small medieval castle, the stronghold of the Catalan mercenaries who dominated this part of Greece in the 13th century AD, overlooks Ámfissa, on the shore of the 'sea of olives' which covers the plain below Delphi. North of the plain, the sharp-peaked 2,510m Gióna (Gionia) massif rises steeply. There are quaint 18th-century streets around the old *platia*, overlooked by the pine-clad castle peak.
8km northwest of Delphi.

ANDÍRRION

A squat Venetian fortress guards the busy pier of this port on the narrowest part of the Gulf of Corinth. On the south shore of the gulf, its twin guards the harbour of Rion.
12km west of Navpaktos.
Ferries run at 15–30-minute intervals between the two, linking Patras and the Peloponnese with the northern mainland.

GALAXÍDHION

Galaxidhion is one of the gems of the Gulf coast, a charming town on a headland between two sheltered bays. Tall 19th-century mansions, fishing boats and seafood restaurants crowd the waterfront below a huddle of pretty balconied houses rising to the dome of a grand 19th-century church built by one of the town's many prosperous shipowners, all reflected in the mirror of the double harbour. If Galaxídhion had a beach it would be perfect; even without one it is one of the pleasantest stops on this coast.

25km southwest of Delphi.

ITÉA

Itéa offers the only beaches of any kind for around 30km in either direction, with a short crescent of pebbles at the east end of its eucalyptus-lined esplanade and a second stretch of grey sand and pebble beach just around the corner. Otherwise, Itéa fails to live up to the inspiring backdrop of Parnassós and Gionia behind it and the peaks of Killíni across the Gulf.

12km south of Delphi.

NÁVPAKTOS

Battlements and turrets surround the holiday-postcard harbour of this little port and scramble up through the town centre to enclose a substantial 15th-century Venetian castle among pine trees on the hill above.

Behind the harbour, a huge flagstoned square is shaded by pines and plane trees and cluttered with café tables. A busy modern town stretches either side of the old-fashioned centre.

160km west of Levádhia.

THE BATTLE OF LEPANTO

On 7 October 1571 a Turkish fleet of 200 galleys commanded by Ali Pasha sailed from Návpaktos – then called Lepanto – to do battle with the fleet of the Holy League, an alliance of Venetian, Spanish, Genoese, Neapolitan and Papal forces. These had been called together by the Pope to defend Christendom from Turkey's westward surge, and the fleet was commanded by Don John of Austria, bastard son of the Holy Roman Emperor Charles V.

Among the Christian combatants were Miguel de Cervantes (1547–1616), author of the comic epic *Don Quixote*, who lost the use of his left hand in the battle, and the Genoese commander Giovanni Andrea Dorea. Although outnumbered by the Turkish galleys, Don John's fleet shattered the century-old myth of Ottoman invincibility by destroying 200 Turkish ships while losing 10 of his own, and halted Turkish expansion westward for a generation.

The town of Galaxídhion prospered in the 19th century

THE WESTERN STEREA

AKHELÓÖS
The Akhelóös river, one of Greece's largest, meets the Ionian Sea in a wide fertile delta whose vast expanse of channels and reedbeds is gradually giving way to maize and cotton fields. The delta is a haven for waterbirds. Kingfishers streak along the riverbanks, egrets stalk among the salt-pans and fish traps lining the marshy shore, and storks nest in treetops and on the chimneys and telephone poles of local villages. The delta, a paradise for birdwatchers, is threatened by encroaching cultivation and by plans for further damming of the Akhelóös, whose northern reaches are already blocked by hydro-electric dams.

The Akhelóös river meets the sea in a vast spread of channels and reedbeds – a haven for waterbirds

Access by dirt roads west of Katokhí, 21km from Mesolóngion, where the river's mighty main channel is crossed by the main Mesolóngion–Astakós road.

ASTAKÓS
Looking west to the island of Itháki (Ithaca), this tranquil harbour at the end of a long, narrow inlet dotted with desert islands offers little excitement, though a colourful sunset can be enjoyed from the comfort of a café seat on its taverna-lined esplanade.
50km northwest of Mesolóngion.

MESOLÓNGION (Missolonghi)
Missolonghi's famous lagoon, a patchwork of fish farms and salt pans, is spectacular when seen from the causeway which links the mainland town with its island suburb of Tourlida, a haphazard collection of fishing shacks with a handful of summer-only fish tavernas. The historic town itself was much damaged in World War II.
35km west of Andírrion.

Pili Exodhou (Gate of the Exodus)
Passing through what remains of the city walls, the gate is famed for the sortie made by 9,000 defenders of the city, women and children, in a desperate attempt to escape their Turkish besiegers in April 1826, during the War of Independence. They were betrayed, and fewer than 2,000 escaped to Ámfissa, 80km away. The last defenders blew up their powder magazine to take as many of their attackers with them as possible.
Signposted.

Astakós bay

Iroon Kipos (Park of the Heroes)
Next to the Gate of the Exodus, with
modern statues of Byron and the Greek
leader Markos Botzaris and other heroes
of the 1821–30 war.

MÍTIKAS

So many islands dot the Ionian Sea off
Mítikas that this undiscovered one-street
village with its 3km sweep of white
pebble beach seems to be on a
landlocked lake. Kalamos, the biggest of
them, is only 500m offshore and a small
ferry plies between the village and the
handful of houses on the pine-covered
island, where the battlements of a tiny
16th-century fortress overlook the bay.
84km northwest of Mesolóngion.

VÓNITSA

A huge castle squats above the silvery
waters of the Amvrakic Gulf, overlooking
the naturally sheltered harbour and
esplanade at Vónitsa, a clutter of two-
and three-storey Italianate houses and a
stretch of pebbly beach. The 16th-
century fortress was built by the
Venetians to control the passage into the
Gulf, an enormous mirror-like lagoon
dotted with uninhabited islets.
_120km northwest of Mesolóngion The castle
is unenclosed._

Lord Byron aged 19

BYRON AT MISSOLONGHI
The Romantic poet George Gordon,
Lord Byron (1788–1824), is
remembered all over Greece in
squares and street names, his name
Hellenicized as Vironos. Always an
admirer of Greece and an
enthusiastic supporter of Greek
independence, he landed at
Missolonghi in January 1824
determined to fight for the Greek
cause and was elected its
commander in chief. Before his
complete lack of military experience
could do any damage, however, he
died in April of fever. Ironically, his
untimely death helped to rally
European opinion behind the Greek
struggle. He probably did Greece
more good as a dead hero than as a
live commander.

Arákhova, Delphi, Ámfissa and Galaxídhion

This tour takes in a cross-section of countryside from the pretty mountain village of Arákhova on the slopes of Parnassós to Galaxídhion on its bay of islands. *Allow 5 hours.*

1 ARÁKHOVA

Perched on the shoulder of the 2,457m high Mount Parnassós at a height of 900m, Arákhova has great views and in winter is popular with skiers visiting the mountain's pistes. In summer it is pleasantly cool.

For 10km west of Arákhova the road snakes down the north side of a deep valley with olive terraces below and bare mountain slopes

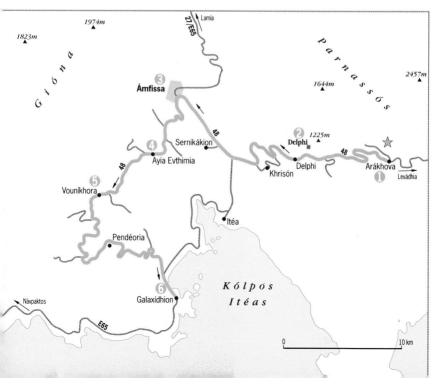

above. After 8km you will get your first glimpse of the Gulf of Corinth ahead, and after a further 1km the columns of the Temple of Apollo at Delphi come into sight. Allow at least 3 hours for Delphi's sites and museums (see pages 88–9).

2 DELPHI

Modern Delphi exists solely to service visitors to the ancient sanctuary. Its two parallel main streets are packed with hotels and uniformly mediocre restaurants.

The road hairpins down towards the sea until, 5km below Delphi, it passes beneath itself in a tight loop and bridge. Follow signs for Itéa and Ámfissa. After 5km you reach the fringes of the 'sea of olives' and continue for 10km through the groves to Ámfissa.

3 ÁMFISSA

This unassuming little town is crowned by a pretty 13th-century castle among pines on a crag. Built by Franks and Catalan mercenaries, it incorporates remnants of the earlier classical acropolis. The walls surround the remains of a keep, round tower, chapel and barracks.

Leave the town by Odos Ethniki Antistasi, which runs from the south side of Ámfissa's main square, and climb in zigzags for 5km, leaving the olive-groves behind, and emerge suddenly on bare hillside with the rocky peak of Gionia on the northern skyline. The road skirts the flank of the Gionia massif, trending south towards the Gulf of Corinth.

4 AYIA EVTHIMIA (AYIA ETHIMIA)

Set among fields and almond trees, Ayia Ethimia is an attractive old-fashioned village of red-tiled stone houses. This part of the drive is especially pretty in spring, when the fields are vivid with wild

flowers, and in autumn, when the almond orchards turn a brilliant red.

5 VOUNÍKHORA (VOUNIHORA)

The village is surrounded by a distinctive maze of grey dry-stone sheepfold walls. The road now climbs steeply over barren slopes with fine views to the north and of Parnassós with Delphi and Arákhova perched on its flanks to the east.

The whole Gulf of Corinth panorama comes into view 2km beyond Vouníkhora and after a further 3km you turn left, following signs to Pendéoria and Galaxídhion in a series of hairpins until you meet the main coast road 1km east of Galaxídhion. The turn-off to the village is on the inland side of the highway and passes beneath the main road.

6 GALAXÍDHION

A substantial domed church, built in the last century by one of Galaxídhion's wealthy shipowners, surmounts this pretty village on a headland at the mouth of the Kólpos Itéas (Gulf of Itéa). With its double harbour, fishing boats, yachts, fish restaurants and waterfront dominated by tall, elegant 19th-century houses, Galaxídhion seems to belong more to the islands than the mainland. It lacks only a beach to make it perfect.

Wealthy shipowners' mansions from Galaxídhion's 19th-century heyday

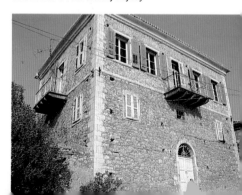

Ípiros and Thessalía

(Epirus and Thessaly)

*T*he two regions which make up the central part of the northern mainland could hardly be more different.

In the west, the Píndhos mountains which form the spine of Epirus conceal some of the wildest and most beautiful country in Europe, sheltering Greece's last remaining bears, wolves, griffon vultures and other endangered species. The Píndhos's eastern slopes descend steeply to the rolling farmlands of Thessaly, the richest agricultural land in Greece.

These are regions of climatic extremes, too. The Píndhos summits, reaching heights of more than 2,600m, are snowbound for up to five months, while Europe's highest summer temperatures have been recorded on the plains of Thessaly. Some of Greece's most picturesque mountain villages are to be found in the Zagória region of Epirus and on the Pelion peninsula of Thessaly. Other highlights of central Greece include the old-fashioned towns of Ioánnina and Metsovo and the cliff-top monasteries of the Metéora, and there are fine beaches on both Epirus's Ionian coast and Thessaly's Aegean shores.

Below, left: chestnuts are an important cash crop on the Pelion peninsula
Right: the Píndhos mountain range

EPIRUS AND THESSALY

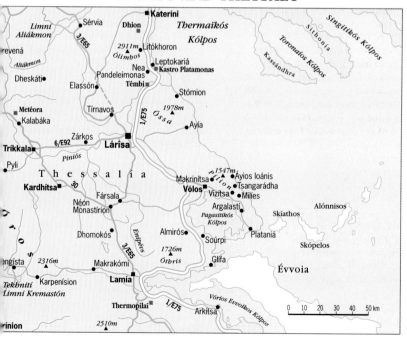

Roussanou monastery; the interior contains a fine fresco of the Last Judgement

inhabited, some of them by a solitary monk or nun. Two – Ayia Triadha and Ayios Stefanos – are functioning monastic houses, while the rest are preserved as religious museums.

Ayios Nikolaos (Saint Nicholas)

Ayios Nikolaos is a recently-restored 14th-century monastery whose 16th-century chapel is decorated with frescos of the Last Judgement by the Cretan painter Theophanes. They are all the more striking for their restoration.

Ayios Stephanos (Saint Stephen)

Now a nunnery, Ayios Stephanos was founded in the 14th century and has two churches, a 14th-century basilica with frescos and a later 18th-century building. The museum houses manuscripts, embroideries and some striking icons.

Ayia Triadha (Holy Trinity)

The 15th-century monastery may look familiar; the James Bond epic *For Your Eyes Only* (1981) was shot here. The building sits atop one of the tallest of the natural pillars.

Mega Meteoron (Great Meteoron)

This is the grandest and most venerable of the monasteries, with a small museum in its 16th-century refectory and well-preserved frescos in the dome of its 15th–16th-century church.

Ossios Varlaam

Ossios Varlaam also has a frescoed chapel and the prettiest flower-gardens of all the monasteries. Here, too, you can see the perilous-looking winch used in the past to haul up monks and visitors as

CENTRAL THESSALY

KALABÁKA (KALAMBAKA)

As you approach Kalambaka, the gentle contours and agricultural patchwork of the Thessalian lowlands start to rise towards the grand highlands of the Píndhos range. Behind the unexciting market town, a blank 555m cliff face rises, a landmark to show you are approaching the unearthly landscape of the Metéora.
21km north of Trikkala.

METÉORA

Nothing prepares you for the scenic impact of this valley lined with soaring towers of rock, each crowned by a precarious monastery. The views over Thessaly and the valley of the upper Piniós are breathtaking. Only six of two dozen monasteries dating from the 14th century are open, and only five are

well as supplies. Its church of Ayioi
Pandes (All Saints) dates from the 16th
century and has perhaps the finest
frescos of all the monastery churches,
including scenes of the Last Judgement
and the life of John the Baptist.

Roussanou

The monastery of Roussanou, with its
red-tiled roof, is dizzyingly located on a
crag which looks ready to topple away
from the cliff face and is reached by a
vertigo-inducing footbridge.

*The valley of the Metéora begins at
Kastraki, 3km from Kalambaka. The trip
taking in all six visitable monasteries is
17km.*
*For all monasteries: (tel: 0432 22278).
Open: hours can vary from monastery to
monastery, but are generally 8am–1pm and
3pm–5pm, sometimes closed on holy days
and religious festivals.*
*Separate admission charge for each
monastery. Dress code: long trousers for
men, skirts below the knee for women, long
sleeves for both.*

MÉTSOVON (Metsovo)

Local costume – typified by the clog-like
shoes with red woollen pom-poms on
sale in every souvenir shop – is dying out
slowly, and you are most likely to see it
worn on feast days. At 1,000m above sea
level, Metsovo is bitterly cold in winter,
so the colourful rugs and blankets which
brighten Metsovo's main-street shops are
no surprise. The view eastward over the
fertile farmlands of Thessaly contrasts
sharply with the hostile peaks of the
Pindhos to the west. Above the town, the
highest pass in Greece (1,705m) carries
the main road between Thessaly and
Epirus.
90km nortrhwest of Trikkala.

Arkhondiko Tositsa (Tositsa Mansion)

The restored 18th-century mansion was
the home of the wealthy Tositsa family,
native philanthropists who also endowed
the nearby Idhrima Tositsa (Tositsa
Foundation).
  Its exhibition includes traditional
costumes and textiles.
*On the main street. Open: daily, except
Thursday, 8.30am–1pm and 4pm–6pm.
Admission charge.*

TRÍKKALA

A dusty market town with a thriving old-
fashioned bazaar area left over from its
heyday as capital of the region under
Turkish rule, Trikkala stands on a low
hill crowned by a crumbling Byzantine
castle and is surrounded by farms.
61km west of Larisa.

The rocky pillars and pinnacles of the Metéora,
which means, appropriately, 'in the air'

PRIESTS, MONKS AND

The bearded village priest in his black robe is a familiar figure

The village priest with his black robe, stovepipe hat and beard is one of the chief characters of any Greek community. Most Greeks feel that to be Greek is to be Orthodox, and the Church helped to keep the flame of Greek language and culture alight during the long centuries of Turkish rule. It is still very much a living religion, and Greece sometimes seems to have more churches than it needs. Even a small village may have two or three churches and chapels – Greeks who were successful overseas or in business have traditionally thanked their patron saint by building a church or chapel in his or her name.

The Greek Orthodox Church moved away from the Western Catholic Church over several centuries, the final split coming in 1074 when the Pope and the Patriarch in Constantinople excommunicated each other. Under the Ottoman Empire, Greece was cut off from the Christian West and the split became permanent. Clerics like Archbishop Germanos of Patras, who declared the start of the

MIRACLES

War of Independence in 1821, were often in the forefront during the many rebellions against the Turks.

Oddly enough, the head (the Patriarch) of the Greek Orthodox Church lives not in Athens but in Istanbul (still called Constantinopolis by Greeks), the last living relic of the great Christian empire of Byzantium. Monks and abbots rank higher in the hierarchy of the Orthodox Church than priests and bishops, but married men may become priests – all those Greek names beginning with 'Papa' indicate a priest roosting somewhere in the family tree.

Sacred relics and centuries-old icons are a vital part of the Orthodox faith and are said to have miraculous powers. No church or chapel, however remote, is ever without its complement of flickering candles, kept alight by the devout.

The Church comes into its own at Easter, the biggest festival of the Greek year, when holy icons are paraded through the streets and solemn services are held by censer-swinging bishops draped in sumptuous silken robes.

ICONS

The finest of Greece's ancient icons have an impact as strong as anything by Picasso. Icons – paintings of Christ, the Virgin, saints or angels – are Greece's direct link with the great Byzantine empire in its heyday. Some are more than a 1,000 years old, but for sheer beauty there is nothing to choose between these and icons painted as late as the 18th and 19th centuries. The style is strict, and the purpose is always to lift the spirit. Authentic icons are virtually impossible to buy, and taking them out of the country is against the law, but several modern icon artists such as Kostas Georgopoulos paint wonderful replicas which are faithful to the original. Georgopoulos uses up to 30 different materials, from silver and gold leaf to natural dyes mixed with egg yolk, animal glues, old hewn boards, and 10 different ageing chemicals.

The Sanctuary of Zeus at Dodona, the oldest sacred site on the mainland

IOÁNNINA AND AROUND

DHODHÓNI (Dodona)

The oldest sacred site on the Greek mainland stands in a remote valley among fields and sees few visitors. Dedicated to the Great Goddess from 2000BC before becoming a sanctuary of Zeus from around 1300BC, the most impressive feature is the theatre with its 45 tiers of seats, restored in the 19th century. Massive walls and column stumps outline the Temple of Herakles and the Sanctuary of Zeus.

21km southwest of Ioánnina, 13km west of the main Ioánnina-Árta road. Signposted. Open: weekdays, 8am–7pm (5pm winter); weekends and holidays, 8.30am–3pm. Admission charge.

IOÁNNINA

Ioánnina's location on pea-green Limni Pamvotis/Límni Ioánninon (Lake Pamvotis), surrounded by rugged peaks, cannot be bettered. A tumbledown bazaar area, a 1,300-year-old walled town, and a handful of mosques and minarets surviving from Turkish times give the town an oriental air.

469km northwest of Athens.

Arkheologiko Mousio (Archaeological Museum)

A well-displayed collection of bronze tools and weapons, stone and bone implements, and finds from Dhodhóni.

Platia 25 Martiou. Signposted. Open: Monday, 12.30pm–7pm; Tuesday to Friday, 8am–7pm; weekends 8.30am–3pm.

Frourion (Fortress)

The fortress town is ringed by walls built in AD528 by the Emperor Justinian against the rampaging Goths. A tree-lined esplanade runs along the lake front. Enter the walls by the Glikidhon gate, off Dionysou Filosofotou just south of the café-filled square below the northeast bastion. Within, a derelict Turkish barracks stands beside a dusty parade-ground.

Dimotikou Mousio (Popular Museum)

Rusting cannon and a pyramid of cannon-balls greet you as you enter the former mosque of Aslan Pasha. Some of the cannon bear the lion crest of the Republic of Venice or the double eagle of the Russian Tsars. There is a fine view of Pamvotis from the square outside the museum. Built in 1618 on the site of a church of St John the Baptist, the mosque was in use until 1922 and became a museum in 1933. Displays include relics and costumes of Ioánnina's Greek, Turkish and Jewish communities.

Alexiou Noutsou. Signposted from the

entrance to the fortress. Open: daily,
8.30am–3pm. Admission charge.

Mousio Laografias (Museum of Folklore)

Silver jewellery, chased brass trays, and
Sarakatsan embroidery and weaving are
displayed with folk costumes in an old
mansion with vividly painted ceilings.
Mihail Angelou 42. Open: Monday to
Wednesday, 10am–1pm. Admission charge.

Tsami Fethye (Victory Mosque)

The derelict mosque, built in 1430,
stands amid ruins in a fortress within a
fortress.
Overlooking Platia Katsandoni. Closed to
the public.

NISSI (Island)

Glass tanks full of live carp, eels, crayfish
and crabs greet visitors to Lake
Pamvotis's only island, a favourite trip
for diners from Ioánnina. Some
restaurateurs keep turtles, salamanders
and even baby alligators – not to eat, but
to catch your eye.

   Five monasteries, the oldest dating
from the 11th century and the most
recent from the 17th, are dotted around
the island.
Boats go to the island from Ioánnina every
half hour (hourly in winter) from the pier on
Dionysou Filosofotou, close to the northeast
corner of the fortress.

Moni Ayios Padeleimonas (Monastery of St Panteleimon)

Small exhibition of books and archives.

Mousio Ali-Pasha (Ali Pasha Museum)

Within the monastery walls, in what were
the monks' cells, a museum of etchings,
watercolours and antiques

commemorates Ali Pasha, the Albanian
warlord who ruled Epirus from 1788
until he was shot in 1822 for rebelling
against the Sultan. You can still see the
bullet-holes in the floor.
Platia Monaxon Nektario-Theofanos.
Open: daily, 8am–8pm. Monastery
museum: admission free. Ali Pasha
museum: admission charge. Signposted from
the waterfront.

PÉRAMA SPILIÁ/SPILAION PERAMATOS (Perama Caves)

Greece's largest cave system, accidentally
discovered in 1940, extends for 2km into
the hillside, winding through grottoes full
of twisted spikes and spires.
In the centre of Perama village, 5km
northwest of Ioánnina (tel: 0651
81521/81440). Open: daily, 8am–8pm
(4pm in winter). Admission charge.

The former mosque of Aslan Pasha in Ioánnina
is now the town's Popular Museum

Fishing boats moored at the mouth of the Akheronda

THE EPIRUS COAST

AKHERONDA (Acheron River)

A strong-flowing icy stream, the Acheron emerges from a fissure in the mountainside 4km inland from the hamlet of Glyki. It reaches the sea as a wide, turquoise river at Amoudia, where it has created a 500m sandy beach behind which is a broad delta of fields and reedbeds.

3km west of the main coast road.

AMVRAKIKÓS KÓLPOS (Amvrakic Gulf)

A huge, silvery lagoon dotted with uninhabited islands separates Epirus from Sterea Ellas. Shuttle ferries cross its 750m-wide mouth between Préveza and the southern shore. Off the northern cape on which Préveza stands, Octavian and Mark Anthony fought the sea-battle of Aktion (Actium) in 31BC (see Nikópolis). The north shore, between Préveza and Menídhi, is a region of salt-marshes and brackish lagoons which attract migrating birds, but has nothing to offer non-birdwatchers.

ÁRTA

Árta was an important town in Roman and medieval times. Little remains of its former glory except a celebrated 18th-century Turkish bridge across the Arakhthos river, currently being restored. The 13th-century walls incorporate fragments of earlier classical and Hellenistic buildings.

75km south of Ioánnina.

EFIRA NEKROMANTION (Necromanteion of Efyra)

In ancient times the Acheron, also known as the Styx, was thought to flow from the underworld and an Oracle of the Dead stood on what was then an island and is now a low hill surrounded by fields. Pilgrims passed through a labyrinth of corridors to question the priestess, who had to be at least 50 years old. Offerings to Hades and Persephone were lowered into a shrine below, believed to be the upper part of Hades' underground palace. A wall of giant blocks surrounds the site, where a small Byzantine church with frescos of the Virgin and saints stands above the chamber of the oracle. A small square Turkish keep is now the caretaker's office.

1km from Amoudia on the main coast road, signposted (tel: 0681 41026). Open: daily, 8.30am–3pm.

IGOUMENÍTSA

The only reason for visiting this characterless seaport close to the Albanian border is to catch a ferry to Corfu or Italy.

101km west of Ioánnina.

NIKÓPOLIS

Scattered over a vast area, brick and stone walls, gateways and the arches of an aqueduct rise from the woods and fields. Two small archaeological sites are enclosed, but the most impressive part of Nikópolis and the best place from which to view the whole site is the theatre, accessible at any time. The stadium, opposite the theatre, is overgrown and indistinguishable to any but the most experienced eye. The site is powerfully evocative of lost glories. Built by Octavian, the future Roman Emperor Augustus, to mark his victory over Mark Anthony and Cleopatra at Aktion (31BC) the city was abandoned in 1040 after being sacked by the Bulgars.

8km north of Preveza.
Archaeological site. Signposted. Open: daily, except Monday, 8.30am–3pm. Admission charge.

Roman ramparts at the lost city of Nikópolis, abandoned in AD1040

PÁRGA

Once a Venetian harbour, Párga is a lively holiday resort. Rows of brightly painted houses climb from a crescent bay dotted with islands to a hill crowned by a Venetian castle. North of this headland stretches a 1km sandy beach. There are smaller beaches either side of the headland at the south end of the bay, and others can be reached by motorboats which run frequently throughout the day in summer.

50km north of Préveza.

Kastro (Castle)

The walls surround an inner ring of battlements and a 13th-century keep where rusting cannon lie scattered.
Open: daily, 8am–8pm (5pm in winter). Admission free.

PRÉVEZA

There are adequate beaches a few kilometres northwest of town, but Préveza offers little else to the holidaymaker. The main road turns inland towards Párga, and shuttle ferries cross the mouth of the Amvrakic Gulf to the Sterea Ellas shore.
125km south of Ioánnina.

Rocky islands punctuate the bay in front of the whitewashed buildings of Párga

The Piniós river passes through the Vale of Tempe, a strategic pass since the earliest times

LÁRISA, ÓSSA AND THE VALE OF TEMPE

LÁRISA

A town of few charms, Lárisa's importance as a road junction in medieval times is reflected by a frowning medieval castle on a central hilltop overlooking the Piniós river, which flows through the town. Lárisa stood guard over routes north, south, east and west. Today, it is bypassed by National Road 1, which turns northeast from the city to enter the Vale of Tempe.
318km north of Athens.

ÓSSA

Like a mountain in a child's story, Óssa stands alone, its often cloud-capped peak rising sharply from the cotton fields of the Thessalian plain. Rising to 1,978m, Óssa is dwarfed by its giant neighbour, the 2,917m Olimbos (Olympus) not far to the north. A logging road, more suitable for four-wheel-drive vehicles than for saloon cars, runs from the hill hamlet of Spili over the shoulder of the mountain to the sea, with vertiginous

views of misty canyons, forest slopes, and the Olympus massif.

The Greek Alpine Society (EOS) maintains a mountain shelter closer to the summit for those who want to trek to the top of the peak.

GODS V GIANTS

While Zeus and the other Olympians were still consolidating their hold on the world after overthrowing Cronus and the other Titans, they faced a revolt by the serpent-footed Giants, brothers of the Titans. Led by Alcyoneus, the 24 giants tried to assault Olympus, the home of the gods, by placing Mount Pelion on Mount Óssa to make a stairway, but were defeated thanks to Heracles, who slew their leader, and Athene, who showed the Olympians a magic herb which made them invulnerable.

STÓMION

Stómion is a quiet harbour-cum-resort

close to the mouth of the Piniós river, where lagoons, channels and reedbeds shelter storks, kingfishers, herons and other waterbirds. A sandy, deserted beach runs north for several kilometres. The green slopes of Óssa to the south and the bare, cloud-capped Olympus to the north make a breathtaking backdrop.
40km northeast of Larisa.

VALE OF TEMPE

The Piniós river flows from its source in the Píndhos mountains across the plain of Thessaly before passing through the once-romantic Vale. A strategic pass since the dawn of time, the deep, 12km gorge in classical times formed a natural barrier between the Greece of the southern city-states and the wilder, less civilized lands of the northern Hellenes. It now carries National Road 1 as well as the main Athens–Thessaloníki rail line and is marred by fumes and noise. Prominently signposted, the Spring of Aphrodite and the Spring of Dafni, which flow into the Piniós, have been reduced to smelly culverts.

Ayia Paraskevi

Midway along the Vale of Tempe, a large lay-by offers the chance to pull off the road and view the Piniós river, crossed here by a suspension bridge. A more attractive view of the river and the great valley is offered by the small motor cruisers which operate half-hour, 4km cruises on the river, departing when full (about every 30 minutes).
On OE1 (National Road 1), 4km south of the tollbooth at the north end of the Vale of Tempe.

Kastro Platamonas (Platamon Castle)

The fortress founded in 1204 by Boniface de Montferrat, Duke of Thessaloníki, was added to by the Byzantines in the 14th and 15th centuries and later by the Turks. Squatting close to the mouth of the Vale of Tempe, it guards the strategic route between northern and southern Greece. The walls are some 7m high, with round bastions at each corner. The octagonal inner keep is being restored and is used for performances during the annual Olympus Festival.
East of the main road on a hilltop opposite the modern village of Nea Pandeleimonas, signposted. Open: daily, except Monday, 8.30am–3pm. Admission charge.

The Vale of Tempe, where according to myth the nymph Daphne was changed into a laurel tree by her earth-mother to save her from Apollo's amorous advances

The Vikos Gorge. Agility and a head for heights are essential requirements for the gorge trail

OCHI DAY
On 28 October 1940 the Italian ambassador presented General Ioannis Metaxas, then military dictator of Greece, with an ultimatum: allow Italian troops to move through Greece to attack the British in Egypt. Metaxas is said to have answered with one word, 'Ochi' (No), and 28 October, a national holiday, is still known as Ochi Day. The Italians invaded immediately, but were turned back by the outgunned but determined Greeks, who delayed an invasion until the arrival of the German forces in April 1941.

THE NORTHERN PÍNDHOS

DRAKOLIMIN
Close to the 2,000m contour, a clear tarn at the lip of a 500m sheer drop is the home of thousands of brightly coloured newts and fire-bellied toads. It is a stiff 8-hour round trip from Mikro Pápingo, calling for above-average fitness and good boots, but well worth it.
5km east and 800m above Mikro Pápingo.

FÁRANX VÍKOS (Vikos Gorge)
The plunge into the 13km-long, 1km-deep gorge cut by the Voïdhomátis river is one of the most dramatic – and demanding – hikes in Greece. The walk takes a full day and is only for the very fit, as you must scramble over boulders and up steep zigzag paths.

In late spring, the gorge may be inaccessible as melting snow turns the Voïdhomátis into an ice-cold torrent.
The gorge runs northwest from Monodhendhri to Megalo Pápingo.

KALPAKION
Polemiko Mousio Kalpáki (Kalpáki War Museum)
The museum's motley collection of elderly rifles, machine-guns, uniforms and other militaria commemorates Greece's against-all-odds victory over the Italian invaders here in the winter of 1940. Opposite the museum is a monument to General Ioannis Metaxas.
On the east side of the main north-south highway, 500m south of Kalpakion village, 35km north of Ioánnina. Open: daily, 8am–5pm. Admission free.

KÓNITSA

Bypassed by the main north–south highway, Kónitsa is a quiet, tree-filled, 19th-century town at the upper end of the vast valley of the Aóös river. Above it tower the peaks of Smólikas, Greece's second-highest mountain at 2,637m, and the Timfi massif, rising to 2,497m at its highest.

64km north of Ioánnina.

MONODHÉNDHRI

The stern grey limestone walls and stone-flagged roofs of Monodhéndhri perch on the very lip of the Vikos Gorge. If you do not feel up to walking the full length of the gorge, you can make the tiring but scenic descent to the river bed and back to Monodhéndhri in half a day. Several of the village's solidly-built traditional homes have been turned into comfortable guest-houses as part of the Greek National

The twin villages of Megalo Pápingo and Mikro Pápingo in the Zagória

Tourist Office's traditional settlements programme.

45km northeast of Ioánnina.

PÁPINGO (Megalo and Mikro)

The twin villages of Megalo (Big) and Mikro (Little) Pápingo stand at the northwest end of the Vikos Gorge, dwarfed by the enormous, pitted crags of the Tímfi massif. In the saddle 500m above the upper village of Mikro Pápingo you can see silhouetted the Astraka mountain refuge, a tiring 3-hour walk up very steep paths. Megalo Pápingo is the most popular base for hiking and exploring in the Zagória.

50–51km northeast of Ioánnina.

THE ZAGORIA

The lovely, dramatically sited villages of this mountain region are built and roofed with the same grey stone and seem to grow from the mountains which surround them. Zagória offers the best mountain trekking in Greece, with high ranges separated by deep canyons which are dry in summer but rushing torrents as the winter snow melts. Under Turkish rule, the Zagória villages won certain tax privileges, and many local men went abroad to work, sending money home to build the handsome houses and churches which adorn the mountainsides. Many of the 40-plus villages are deserted, but tourism (a newcomer to the region) is helping to bring them back to life.

The port of Vólos at the head of the Pagasitic Gulf, looked down upon from the Pelion peninsula

VÓLOS AND PÍLION (PELION)

The northern part of the mountainous, boot-shaped Pílion (Pelion) peninsula is watered by many streams and wooded with beech, oak and chestnut and with pear and apple orchards. The toe of the boot is barren and rugged. Pelion is separated from mainland Thessaly by the Pagasitikós Kólpos (Pagasitic Gulf), which laps at sheltered beaches on the west coast of the peninsula. Lush forest covers the slopes of the east coast, which drop steeply to deep blue water and white pebble beaches. Pelion's substantial half-timbered mansions with their slate roofs and elaborate polished wood interiors are among the most beautiful village homes in Greece. Many have been restored thanks to the Greek National Tourist Office's traditional settlements programme (see page 177).

ÁYIOS IOÁNNIS

A relaxed resort with a sweep of steeply shelving, east-facing sand and pebble beach below lush, tropical-looking slopes, Áyios Ioánis is popular with Greek vacationers.
41km east of Vólos.

MAKRINÍTSA

The most accessible of Pelion's villages,

Makrinítsa is also the most affected by tourism. Many traditional homes have been converted into guest-houses. The village stands above a deep valley, its eastern slopes greenly wooded but the western side, only a few hundred metres away, dry and bare.

An arcaded church of Áyios Ioánis Prodhromos (St John the Baptist) stands in a main square sheltered by three enormous plane trees. The urban smear of Vólos, 14km away, dominates the westward view.
14km northwest of Vólos.

MILÍES/MILEAI (Milies)

The frescoed church of Áyios Michaelis o Taxiarchis (St Michael 'the brigadier') stands beside an expansive balconied square with breathtaking views over the green hills of Pelion and across the silver Pagasitic Gulf. Inside the church are apocalyptic murals of saints, angels, sinners and devils. Below the square a derelict railway station awaits the restoration of the Pelion narrow-gauge railway from Vólos.
27km from Vólos.

Mousio Mileai (Milies Museum)

Exhibition of local costume and folkways.

On the main street, above the square (tel: 0423 86204). Open: Tuesday to Sunday and all holidays, 10am–2pm; closed 10–20 March, June and September.

TSANGARÁDHA

Tsangarádha's scattered squares are connected by steep cobbled steps and rushing streams. This is the prettiest of the eastern Pelion villages, looking out over the steep forests towards the silhouette of Skiathos on the eastern horizon. Its landmark is an enormous plane tree, 18m round and said to be 1,000 years old.

38km east of Vólos.

VIZÍTSA

At the end of a steeply winding road from the coast, Vizítsa is built around two huge flagstoned squares under the shelter of enormous plane trees and is full of the sound of running water. Villagers gather at café tables in the afternoon and evening to play backgammon and drink *tsipouro*, a fiery grape spirit.

31km south of Vólos.

VÓLOS

Vólos, the gateway to the Pelion, is Greece's third port after Piraeus and Thessaloníki. A mainly industrial town at the head of the Pagasitic Gulf, it was rebuilt on a rigid grid pattern after being flattened by an earthquake in 1955.

355km north of Athens.

Mousio Arkheologiko (Vólos Archaeological Museum)

Hundreds of Hellenistic tombstones, carved with everyday scenes, are the centrepiece of a collection which also includes Stone Age implements and Mycenaean pottery.

N. Plastira 22 (tel: 0421 25285). Open: daily, except Monday, 8.30am–3pm. Admission charge.

Mousio Theophilou (Theophilos Museum)

This mansion is decorated with vibrant primitive frescos of robbers, priests, pashas and warriors, the work of the self-taught painter Theophilos who spent much of his life roaming the Pelion.

Off Eleftherias, Nea Vólos (tel: 0421 430 88). Open: 8.30am–3pm. Admission free.

Sidherodhromo Piliou (Pelion Railway)

The narrow-gauge tracks you can see weaving along Vólos's waterfront and out of town towards Pelion are a relic of the Pelion railway, built in the last century. Two tiny locomotives and their miniature carriages can be seen rusting in sidings at the main railway station.

Fresco of the Archangel Michael at the church in Milies which bears his name

Villages of Zagória

The stone-built villages of the Zagória region with their grey-slabbed roofs stand among the most exciting mountain scenery in Greece. Tourism is a relative newcomer, encouraged by newly built roads. The region is traversed by deep canyons, crossed in many places by graceful arched bridges built without the use of mortar. Wildlife abounds. Look out for griffon vultures circling the high peaks and for tortoises crossing the road. *Allow 6 hours.*

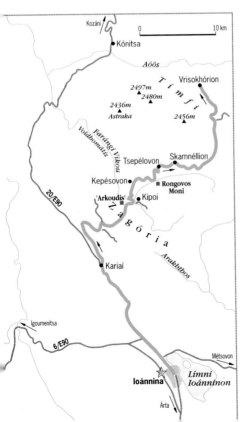

The drive starts 18km north of Ioánnina, leaving the main Ioánnina-Kónitsa road at Kariaí and following the signposted road towards Tsepélovon. Continue to follow the Tsepélovon signs at each junction.

ARKOUDIS MEMORIAL

Twenty-six kilometres from the Kariaí junction, a roadside plaque commemorates the guerrilla leader Yioryios Arkoudis, 'killed by a Turkish bullet' here in 1906 when this part of Greece was still under the rule of the Turks.

A modern bridge crosses the confluence of two river beds 1km further on. A steeply arched old bridge stands next to it, between sheer cliff walls. You are now entering the heart of the Zagória canyon country. The river bed, dry for most of the year, becomes a torrent in winter and early spring.
The road climbs for 8km towards Kepésovon, perched on the lip of the canyon.

KIPOI (KIPI)

Before reaching Kepésovon, you can turn right and detour for 4km to the village of Kipoi, to view the triple-arched

The three-arched bridge at Kipi is the finest of the Zagória pack-bridges

bridge crossing the ravine 1km west of the village.

Just after the Kepésovon turning, pull off the road and look across the gorge to where a little-used mule path zigzags perilously down the cliff face. These cobbled paths, most of which have fallen into disrepair with the building of modern roads, were the highways of the region. *Drive for another 5km.*

RONGOVOS MONASTERY

The monastery and church of Ayios Ioannis are well worth the 10-minute walk from the road, even if a monkish caretaker is not in residence. The view into the canyon below is breathtaking. *3km beyond the monastery and 30km from the main Ioánnina-Kónitsa road, Tsepélovon is the biggest and most atmospheric of the Zagória villages.*

TSEPÉLOVON

Two gigantic plane trees shade a flagstoned square, Platia Stratigou Tsakalotou Thrasyvoulou, and its three old-fashioned cafés. At one end of the square stands a six-sided stone clock tower built in 1868 and behind it is the attractive colonnaded church of Ayios Nikolaos, built in 1871 and lavishly decorated within. Many of Tsepélovon's older houses are derelict, but are being restored.

From Tsepélovon the road passes through pine forests to Skamnéllion, then through alpine scenery for some 15km below limestone peaks, sparsely covered with pine trees, before dropping to the red-roofed village of Vrisokhórion.

VRISOKHÓRION (VRISOHORI)

Built on either side of a fertile, sheltered valley, the village is a mountain oasis of garden terraces and walnut trees among oak woods. The substantial arcaded church of Ayios Xaralampos with its carved stone doorway is typical of Zagória village churches.

A bulldozed road, suitable only for four-wheel-drive vehicles and experienced off-road drivers, ends 3km from Vrisokhórion at the bottom of a steep canyon. When this book was being researched a concrete road bridge was being built with the aim of connecting Vrisokhórion with Kónitsa.

GOATS AND GOATHERDS

The tinkling of goatbells across a silent mountain valley is one of the unforgettably evocative sounds of Greece. Nobody whose car has been stopped and surrounded by a herd of goats being driven across the road will forget the smell, either.

The goat, like the forest fire, played its part in the deforestation of Greece, reducing most mountainsides to barren, rocky terrain that only a goat could love.

Like everything else in Greece, the goat is a political issue, with environmentalists condemning a 1980s government decision to allow grazing on national forest land devastated by fire – a move which may perhaps have encouraged firebugs to burn off still more trees for goat pasture.

The goat is still central to survival for many mountain villagers, and herders drive their flocks from lower slopes into the high peaks in summer to take advantage of pastures watered by melting snow.

Hill-walkers will meet goatherds in the most unpromising-looking locations, and their corrals of dry-stone walls, thorns, and corrugated iron (called *stanes*) are useful landmarks in the Greek high country.

Many of the goatherds who pasture their flocks in the Píndhos mountains of northern Epirus are Vlachs, members of a dwindling ethnic minority who speak a language closely related to Romanian, and whose ancestors are said to have been Roman legionaries who guarded the mountain passes in ancient times.

Others are descended from the Sarakatsan clans, who until the early years of this century lived a truly nomadic existence. You can see their colourful rugs and embossed silver jewellery in many of the region's folk museums.

Goat meat rarely turns up on tourist menus, and even in Greek homes it is a dish for special occasions such as as Easter and Panayiria, the feast of the Assumption of the Virgin (15 August).

Greek goats find a meal wherever they can

Makedhonía and Thráki

(Macedonia and Thrace)

Greece's northernmost provinces border Bulgaria, Turkey and the former Yugoslav republic of Macedonia, and their remoter regions are still comparatively untouched by the modern world.

Macedonia, hemmed in to the west and south by the great mountain ranges of the north Píndhos and Olympus, has a strong identity of its own. Its people are often taller and fairer than their southern compatriots and are often blue- or grey-eyed. Their huge province includes fertile valleys watered by Greece's biggest rivers, huge lakes, the highest mountain in Greece, the country's second city and – on the triple peninsulas of Khalkidhikí – a self-governing theocracy and some of the country's best and as yet totally unspoilt beaches.

Thrace, lying further east, clearly shows its Turkish heritage in the music, dress, arts and crafts of its large Muslim minority. Its flat coastal plain shimmers in the summer sun, growing bumper crops of grain, cotton and tobacco, minarets shoot skyward from many of its sleepy villages, and storks and pelicans haunt the reedbeds and lagoons along its coast. Of all the regions of Greece, Thrace is the least touched by tourism, depending for its livelihood instead on agriculture. In these flat farmlands the traditional two-wheeled donkey cart is still one of the most popular means of transport.

A combination of little-visited towns

WHAT'S IN A NAME?

With the break-up of Yugoslavia, Greece claimed sole rights to the name Macedonia and did everything it could to block recognition of the province's northern neighbour, the former Yugoslavian republic of Macedonia, as the Republic of Macedonia. Though the campaign seems to have been lost, it is still a touchy subject and, like other topics which touch on the fierce Greek national pride, best avoided.

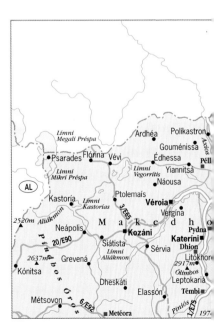

The commercial port of Kavala, surmounted by its Byzantine castle

and villages and some splendid rugged mountain country in the north of the region makes Thrace one of Greece's best-kept secrets.

MACEDONIA AND THRACE

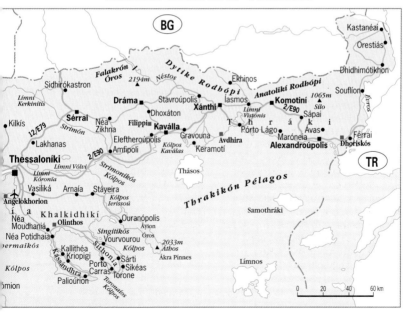

EASTERN MACEDONIA AND THRACE

AMFIPOLI (Amfipolis)

The fortifications of this impressive 5th-century BC city are being excavated and restored, as are the mosaic floors of its Christian basilica.

Between Amfipolis and the coastal highway, overlooking the Strimón (Strimonas) river, stands a monumental stone lion, pieced together in 1937 from fragments recovered from the river bed. It dates from the late 4th century BC.
Signposted north of the Kavala-Thessaloníki highway, 60km southwest of Kaválla (Kavala). Unenclosed.

ÉVROS DELTA

The Évros drains into a wide delta of salt lagoons and sluggish channels where seabirds, including pelicans, abound.
13–15km east of Alexandroúpolis. Turn off the main road at Loutra Traianopolis on to a network of dirt roads.

FILIPPI (Philippi)

The most impressive survivals of this town founded in the 4th century BC are the broad, paved expanse of the Roman agorá and the arches and columns of the Christian basilica, begun in the 6th century but never completed because it was too big to support its dome. The town is particularly famous because it was here that Octavian (the future Roman Emperor Augustus) and Mark Anthony defeated Brutus and Cassius, the murderers of Julius Caesar, in 42BC, and because it was at Philippi that the Apostle Paul established the first Christian community in Europe.

On the opposite side of the road is a theatre, carved out of the hillside in the 4th century BC and now used for performances in summer, and the remains of another basilica, built in about AD500.
18km northwest of Kaválla.

KAVÁLLA (KAVALA)

Turkish-style houses with shutters, tiled roofs and overhanging second storeys clutter the winding cobbled streets which ascend from Kavala's busy commercial harbour to its Byzantine castle. The Apostle Paul landed here on his first missionary journey to Europe, and it was here that Mehmet Ali (1769–1849) was born, who became Pasha of Egypt and whose last descendent as ruler of Egypt was King Farouk (abdicated 1952).
170km east of Thessaloníki.

Anapsihtirio Imaret (Turkish Almshouse)

A forest of domes and chimney-pots marks this derelict building above the harbour. Built to house the poor of the city by Mehmet Ali, its cool courtyard with its whitewashed arcades is now a pleasant café-bar adorned with relics of old Kavala.
Opposite junction of Theod Poulidou and Mohamet-Ali.

Arkheologiko Mousio (Kavala Archaeological Museum)

Finds include delicate polychrome glass vases, reliefs and mosaics from Amfipolis, gilded jewellery and a restored 250BC Macedonian tomb chamber.
Erithrou Stavrou (tel: 051 222335), at the western end of the harbour esplanade, in a small park, signposted. Open: daily, except Monday, 8.30am–3pm. Admission charge.

Kastro (Castle)

The Byzantine citadel was taken over and expanded by the Turks. An impressive aqueduct, which supplied the

citadel and the town below with water, crosses the main Kavala-Alexandhroupolis road below the castle.
Open: daily, 9am–3pm. Admission free.

KOMOTINÍ

A quaint mixture of modern and traditional, Komotiní is a market town with a strong ethnic Muslim element. Look out for women in chador-like black dresses and headscarves and older men in soft skullcaps in the open-air market held every Tuesday. The bazaar area in the street either side of pedestrianised Venizelou is fascinating.
113km east of Kaválla.

Mousio Morphotikou Omilou Komotinis (Museum of Folk Life and History)

Collection of domestic items and folk costumes, with fine examples of local wedding embroidery.
Ayiou Yioryiou 13. Open: daily, except Sunday, 10am–1pm.

Yeni Came (Yeni Mosque)

The mosque and its graceful minaret stand next to a 19th-century clock tower bearing an inscription from the Koran.

Behind the mosque stand the headstones and tombs of a Turkish graveyard.
Venizelou 83/Platia Ifaistou.

XÁNTHI

Xánthi's wealth traditionally came from tobacco trading, and its prosperity is reflected by the large mansions built by well-off tobacco factors in its old quarter, many now restored.
56km east of Kaválla.

Laografiko Mousio (Folk Art Museum)

The museum is housed in a splendidly decorated tobacco baron's house with painted ceilings. Displays include weapons, copper and brassware, and gorgeous Sarakatsan rugs.
Antika 7. Open: Monday, Wednesday, Thursday and weekends, 11am–1pm and 6.30pm–8.30pm. Admission charge.

Palaio Xánthi (Old Xánthi)

The old quarter, with its largely car-free cobbled streets and yellow and white stuccoed houses, stands above the modern town centre.
North of Vasilissis Sofias.

A restored tobacco trader's mansion in Xánthi's old quarter

A 14th-century towered fortress guards the harbour at Ouranópolis

KHALKIDHIKÍ

Shaped like a three-fingered hand, Khalkidhikí points south into the Aegean. The easternmost peninsula, closed to tourists, is Áyion Óros (Holy Mountain/Mount Athos), a semi-independent territory ruled by the abbots of its score of monasteries (see the Mount Athos tour, pages 130–1) and dominated by the sharp-edged peak of Athos, 2,033m high, on its southern tip.

Kassándhra, the furthest west of the three peninsulas and the closest to Thessaloníki's international airport is, not surprisingly, the biggest tourism puller, with a necklace of resorts catering to holidaymakers from all over Europe. It is worth spending one night on the west coast for the glowing sunsets, with the peaks of Olympus, Óssa and Pílion (Pelion) silhouetted on the opposite shore of the Thermaïkós Kólpos (Thermaic Gulf), some 50–60km away.

Sithonía (Sidhonia), the middle peninsula, is less developed and more rugged than its western neighbour. Thick pine forest alternates with bare boulders and the scars of forest fires. Sidhonia's east coast has some of the best and least crowded beaches in Greece. Its southern tip is barren and blasted by winter gales and summer heat.

NÉA FÓKAIA

The small square keep of Ayios Pavlos (St Paul) guards a pleasant, east-facing sandy beach with three summer tavernas.
8km south of Néa Potidhia on Kassándhra's east coast. The tower is not open.

NÉA POTÍDHAIA (Nea Potidhia)

The gateway to Kassándhra, where a narrow canal has been cut through the isthmus to allow yachts to pass through.
80km southeast of Thessaloníki.

OLINTHOS

An extensive complex of walls and pits on a flat-topped hill marks the site of ancient Olinthos, destroyed by Philip II of Macedon, father of Alexander, in 348BC. He did a thorough job.
North of the main road, 4km west of Néa Moudhaniá and 1km from the village of Nea Olinthos (tel: 0371 91280). Open: daily, except Monday, 8.30am–3pm.

OURANÓPOLIS

The departure-point for cruises around the Ayion Óros and for pilgrims heading for the monasteries is a bustling little port with a pretty location on the Singitikós Kólpos/Kólpos Ayiou Orous (Gulf of the Holy Mountain). You can hire a boat to explore the small islands offshore. Ferries run frequently to Amoliani, the island opposite the harbour. A 14th-century fortress tower guards the harbour.

10km south of the isthmus linking the Ayion Óros to the mainland.

PALIOÚRION (Paliouri)

A chain of beach resorts runs up the east coast of Kassándhra from Paliouri, close to the peninsula's southern tip. There are many good sandy beaches with a backdrop of pine-clad hills, and the scenery is outstanding.

58km south of Néa Moudhania.

PETRALONA

Halfway between Thessaloníki and Kassándhra are the beautiful stalagmite and stalactite caves of Petralona, with colours ranging from pure white to deep red. The caves were inhabited in palaeolithic times, and contain the earliest known traces of man-made fire, dated to 700,000 years ago.

North of Eleohoria, on the N. Kalikratitia – N. Moudhaniá road. Open: Tuesday to Sunday, 8.30am–3pm. Admission charge.

PORTO CARRAS

A self-contained complex of four enormous, obtrusive and charmless hotels overlooking a yacht marina, riding centre and golf course.

Midway along the west coast of Sidhonia.

SÁRTI

A small resort popular with holidaymakers from Thessaloníki, Sárti stands by a sandy beach at the mouth of a green valley. Lots of tavernas and discos indicate an active nightlife in summer.

On the east coast of Sidhonia, about 30km from its southern tip.

SIKÉAS (Sikias)

A triangle of farmland forms a fertile oasis of fields and orchards hemmed in by low, jagged hills behind a long curve of sandy, little-visited beach.

On the east coast of Sidhonia, about 20km from the southern tip.

TORONE (Toroni)

Toroni could not be more different from its big neighbour. This tiny resort has 2km of sandy beach on a wide west-facing bay, with a backdrop of barren, rocky hills.

5km south of Porto Carras.

VOURVOUROU

Vourvourou is set on a shallow, almost landlocked lagoon overlooking a calm bay with a scattering of tiny islands. There are sandy beaches either side of the small village.

On the east coast of Sidhonia, close to its northern end.

Yachts at anchor in Porto Carras marina on the Sidhonia peninsula

THESSALONÍKI

Greece's second city was largely destroyed by fire in 1917 and struck by an earthquake in 1978, so it comes as some surprise that so many ancient and medieval buildings survive. Built on a long crescent bay at the head of the Thermaïkós Kólpos (Thermaic Gulf), it is a lively city, with smart shops, lots of good restaurants and fashionable cafés, and an energetic nightlife.

Bronze *krater* (wine cauldron) from the 4th century in the Thessaloníki Archaeological Museum

Enter the old quarter at the Dingirle Koule, at the northeast end of Zografou.

APSIS GALERIOU (Arch of Galerius)

The 4th-century arch was built at the crossroads of Roman Thessaloníki to honour the Emperor Galerius. It stands beside one of the city's busiest streets and is being restored.
Corner of Egnatia and Gounari.

AKROPOLIS (Acropolis)

Sections of the city's 4th-century ramparts, extended and reinforced by the Byzantines in the 14th century and the Turks in the 15th, partially enclose the old quarter. The most imposing remnants of the medieval fortifications are the Dingirle Koule (Chain Tower), a twin of the Lefkos Pirgos (White Tówer) on the seafront, and the recently restored section of walls between the Pirgos Palaiologos and the Pirgos Andronikos towers, dating from the 14th century.

ARKHEOLOGIKÓ MOUSÍOU (Archaeological Museum)

The stupendous finds from the royal Macedonian tombs at Vergína (see page 129) are the central attraction of this fine museum. The workmanship and materials testify to the wealth and sophistication of ancient Macedon. Among the most striking are the tiny ivory heads of Philip II and Alexander, beautifully wrought gold jewellery, the embossed gold funerary chests and delicate ornamental wreaths, the bronze, silver and gold shields and cauldrons, and the skeleton of Philip II.
Junction of d'Esperey and Stratou (tel:. 031 830538). Open: Monday, 11am–5pm; Tuesday to Friday, 8am–5pm; weekends and holidays, 8.30am–3pm. Admission charge.

ÁYIOS DHIMÍTRIOS

The church, originally built in the 5th

The White Tower on the waterfront is Thessaloníki's most prominent landmark

century but extensively rebuilt since then, is the largest in Greece. It contains the relics of St Dhimitrios, the city's patron saint, who was executed by the Emperor Galerius at that spot in AD306. *Upper side of Platia Dikastirion (tel: 031 270008). Open: daily, except Monday, 8.30am–3pm. Admission free.*

ÁYIA SOFIA

Like Ayios Dhimitrios, this 8th-century church became a mosque with the Turkish conquest. Now a church again, its dim candlelit interior is decorated with painted domes, restored trompe-l'œil mosaics and richly ornamented screens.
Midway along Egnatia, between Egnatia and Tsimiski. Open: daily, closed 12.30pm–5pm. Admission free.

ÁYIOS YEÓRYIOS/AYIOS YIORGIOS (Rotonda)

The squat, massive building was intended to be the tomb of the Roman Emperor Galerius, was converted into a church in the following century, and became a mosque under the Turks.
Filippou, 50m north of the Apsis Galeriou (Arch of Galerius). Temporarily closed for restoration.

BEDESTAN (Old Market)

The Ottoman-period market area off Venizelou is a chaos of stalls and shops selling everything under the sun. Noisy and colourful, it is a photographer's delight. Go early in the morning to catch it in full swing.

LAOGRAFIKO-ETHNOLOGIKO MOUSION MAKEDHONIAS (Folklife-Ethnological Museum of Macedonia)

A collection of costumes, artefacts, and

The doorway of Thessaloníki's 8th-century church of Áyia Sofia

photographs illustrating the vanished folk art and life of northern Greece, housed in a 19th-century mansion near the waterfront. There is an interesting display on the traditional *karaghiosis* shadow-puppet theatre.
Vass. Olgas 68 (tel: 031 830591). Open: Monday and Wednesday, 9.30am–5.30pm; Tuesday, Friday and Saturday, 9.30am–2pm. Admission charge.

Levkos Pirgos (White Tower)

The 35m circular tower on the waterfront was a bastion of the Byzantine city walls, rebuilt by the Turks in about 1430, and used mainly as a prison. It houses an excellent Byzantine museum with some very striking icons, tombs, mosaics and frescos. The top storey houses a pleasant, cool café whose rooftop terrace offers a fine view of the town and the harbour.
East end of Leoforos Nikis (tel: 031 830538). Open: Monday, 11am–5pm; Tuesday to Friday, 8.30am–5pm; weekends and holidays, 8.30am–3pm. Admission charge.

FISHERMEN

No Greek harbour is complete without its complement of tiny, brightly painted fishing boats and lengths of crimson-dyed net spread out to dry.

Look closely at the prow of many of these little vessels and you will see, cut into the wood, a diamond-shape – a stylised modern version of the painted eye with which the ancient Greeks decorated their galleys.

Most fishing is done at night, and flotillas of one-man craft (sometimes towed behind a larger vessel) usually

Catch of the day.

set out at sundown, to come puttering back with their catch at first light.

Some 5,000 years of intensive fishing have taken their toll of the Aegean's stocks, and Greek boatmen have long used everything from fine-mesh nets to fish-traps and tridents.

In more recent times, dynamite became a potent and popular way of maximising results, and it is not uncommon to meet fishermen who have lost a hand through a mishap with explosives.

With such a comprehensive approach, it is hardly surprising that the catch is increasingly small and mostly made up of tiddlers. Nets full of whitebait, sprats and mackerel are common, but the prized *barbounia* (red mullet) commands a far higher price.

Bigger fish like tunny and swordfish are often caught off the southern Peloponnese, in the deep waters of the Steno Kíthiro (Kithira Channel).

Boats fitted with powerful acetylene lamps are used to attract squid into a circle of nets, while octopus are caught with a trident or a formidable triple hook on a hand-line.

Greece's lakes, too, have their fishing fleets. On Límni Ioánninon (Lake Pamvotis), Límni Kastorías (Lake Kastoria) and the Límni Préspes (Prespa lakes), as well as on the reservoirs formed by Greece's many hydro-electric dams, local fishers set out after carp and other freshwater fish in black-tarred punts.

And on Greece's beaches, fishers of another kind trawl for a different catch: young Greek men who spend their summers in romantic pursuit of female tourists are called *kamaki* – 'harpooners'.

Fishing boat at anchor

Fresh from the Aegean

As the highest mountain in Greece it was only natural that the gods should choose Mount Olympus for their home

and though the beavers which gave it its name *(castor* is Latin for beaver) have disappeared from the area, many small factories still make up the distinctive patchwork fur garments for which the town is known. Grand 19th-century fur-merchants' mansions stand on the slope overlooking the lake, southeast of the modern town centre.
210km west of Thessaloníki.

Koumbelidhiki Panagia
The most important of Kastoría's antique churches has striking exterior frescos of Salome and John the Baptist. Decorative brickwork, interspersing geometric rows of brick with masonry, is a feature of all Kastoría's Byzantine churches.
Off Caravagelli. Closed for renovation.

Laografiko Mousio Kastorias (Kastoría Folk Museum)
On the ground floor of this fur-trader's mansion are barrel-filled cellars, a green courtyard with the kitchen and a copper still. The upper floors have elaborately decorated woodwork, polished floors and painted ceilings.
Kapetan 10. Open: daily, 8.30am–6pm. Admission charge.

WESTERN MACEDONIA

DHION
Highlights of the most impressive site in Macedonia are the marble and mosaic floors of the baths, the Sanctuary of Isis with copies of the original statues, and a length of the cobbled road which led to Olympus.
115km south of Thessaloníki. The site is 2km east of Dhion village (tel: 0351 53206). Open: weekdays, 8am–6pm; weekends and holidays, 8.30am–3pm. Admission charge.

Mousio (Museum)
The museum has a rich and well-displayed collection of statues, coins, jewellery and everyday objects and an excellent explanatory video programme.
In the centre of Dhion village. Signposted. (tel: 0351 53206). Open: Monday, 11am–6pm; Tuesday to Friday, 8.30am–6pm; weekends and holidays, 8.30am–3pm. Admission charge.

KASTORÍA
Surrounded on three sides by its lake, Kastoría is one of the prettiest towns in Greece. It grew wealthy on the fur trade,

Mousio Byzantikon (Byzantine Museum)
The museum's collection of glowing crimson and gold icons is one of the best in Greece. Unfortunately, all texts and explanations are in Greek.
Off V. Iperiou, next to the Xenia hotel. Open: daily, except Monday, 8.30am–3pm. Admission charge.

LÍMNI PRÉSPES (PRESPA LAKES)

Megali Préspa (Great Prespa) and Mikrí Préspa (Little Prespa) are a refuge for pelicans, storks, egrets, spoonbills and cormorants. Around them stand a handful of villages which seem to have been barely touched by the 20th century. *190km northwest of Thessaloníki.*

ÓLIMBOS ÓROS (Mount Olympus)

The tallest mountain in Greece (2,817m) and the legendary home of the gods dominates Macedonia and the north from most angles. The peak is usually covered in cloud by midday, adding to its air of mystery (see Climbing Mount Olympus, page 140).

PÉLLA

The ancient capital of Macedonia, Pélla was also the childhood home of Alexander the Great. Mosaics of warriors in battle, stag hunts, and the abduction of Helen by Paris (see page 59) have been perfectly preserved under layers of silt. Also worth seeing are the columns of the Colonnade of the Court. Excavations are continuing, and a viewing-tower gives you a bird's-eye view of this extensive Macedonian site.

The museum, on the opposite side of the road from the site, has an excellent collection of marbles and some lovely fluid pebble-mosaics and terracotta statuettes.

On the main road between Thessaloníki and Yiannitsá (Yianitsa), 39km west of Thessaloníki (tel: 0382 31160/31278). Open: daily, except Monday, 8.30am–3pm. Admission charge covers site and museum.

VERGÍNA

The tombs identified as those of Philip II of Macedon and other members of his family make this the most significant site unearthed this century. Above ground, the remains of the royal palace include a magnificent mosaic floor with stylised floral and geometric patterns. Below it, the magnificent marble-lined royal tombs with their great stone sarcophagi cannot fail to impress, though the treasures of the tombs – and Philip II's remains – are in the Thessaloníki Archaeological Museum. A smaller tomb, beneath an unsightly metal roof, is between the palace and the village.

Anaktora (Palace): near Palatitsia, 2km from modern Vergína, signposted. Tombs: on the outskirts of Vergína, signposted (tel: 031 830538). Open: daily, except Monday, 8.30am–3pm. Admission charge.

Kastoría and its lake

Áyion Óros (Mount Athos)

Mount Athos, the Holy Mountain, has been ruled by its monks since the 10th century. Special permission from the Ministry of Northern Greece is required to visit the 45km-long peninsula, and women – and even female animals – are banned. Around 1,500 monks now live in the 20 monasteries.

Each monastery is ruled by its abbot and each is built in a distinctively different architectural style. Some perch on the slopes of the mountain, others stand beside natural harbours.

The monasteries of the west coast can be clearly observed from the cruise ships which sail daily from the small port of Ouranópolis, just north of the frontier between the Holy Mountain and the outside world.

Snacks, drinks and camera film are sold on board. Boats must stay at least 500m offshore, so a zoom lens and binoculars are useful. Tickets are sold in advance by agencies on the Ouranópolis harbour-front, and the trip takes 4 to 6 hours. A multi-lingual commentary (English/ German/Greek) is provided.

Leaving Ouranópolis the boat cruises southeast along the barren coast of the peninsula.

DHOKHIARÍOU (DOHIARIOU)

Easily spotted by its crenellated defence tower, this monastery on the seashore was built in the 10th century. It now has around a dozen monks.

XENOFÓNDOS (XENOPHONTOS)

Named after its 10th-century founder, St Xenofon, the fortress-like building overlooks a long pebbly strand.

The 14th-century monastery of Dhionisíou near the peak of Mount Athos

Damaged by pirates and fires, it has frequently been rebuilt and is a patchwork of styles.

AYÍOU PANDELEÍMONOS (AYIOS PANTELEIMONAS)

Most striking and colourful of all, with scarlet walls and green onion-domes, each surmounted by a gold orb and cross, the present monastery was built by Russian monks in the late 18th century.

XIROPOTÁMOU (XEROPOTAMOS)

High on a ridge above the coast, Xiropotámou overlooks the tiny harbour at Dháfni. One of the most modern monasteries, it has been rebuilt a number of times over the last three centuries after a series of disastrous fires.

DHÁFNI (DAFNI)

Below Xiropotámou, Dháfni is the peninsula's official harbour and entry-point for pilgrims. The mountain's only road runs from the port to Kariaí (Karies), the administrative capital of Mount Athos.

SÍMONOS PÉTRAS (SIMONOPETRA)

Perched dizzyingly on its crag, Simonos Pétras is unmistakable, a seven-storey building which seems to grow straight out of the cliff.

OSÍOU GRIGORÍOU (GREGORIOU)

Another clifftop eyrie, Grigoríou is dedicated to St Nicholas and is the smallest of the Athos monasteries. With binoculars you can clearly see its cheerfully colourful red-tiled roof and blue balconies overlooking the sea.

DHIONISÍOU (DIONYSIOU)

The fortress-like 14th-century building is easily recognised by its tiers of white and pink balconies, 80m above the sea. The interior contains some fine frescos.

AYOU PÁVLOU (AYIOS PAVLOS)

High above the sea, Ayiou Pávlou is a dour stone building cradled by outcrops of the peak of Mount Athos.

ÁYION ÓROS (MOUNT ATHOS)

While the whole peninsula is known by this name, the peak itself is at its southern tip. Its steep slopes drop sheer into the sea and the summit towers to a height of 2,033m.

From the southern tip, the boat returns to Ouranópolis.

AMOLIANÍ

Most excursion boats stop at this small island, about 20 minutes from Ouranópolis, where a pretty harbour offers a choice of tavernas. There is a beach about 10 minutes' walk from the harbourside.

Ministry of Northern Greece, Platia Dhikitiriou, Thessaloníki. Permission to visit the holy mountain is usually granted only to Orthodox pilgrims or scholars with a special interest in Greece.

ALEXANDER THE GREAT

Separated from the warring city-states of the southern mainland by mountain ranges, Macedon was thought of by civilised Hellenes as a near-barbarous land.

But the disastrous Peloponnesian War (431–404BC) between Athens and Sparta drew in all the cities of the south and spelt the beginning of the end of their era.

As their political, military and economic power waned, Macedon became a power to be reckoned with.

At the battle of Khairónia in 338BC, (see page 86), Philip II's Macedonians shattered the combined forces of the southern cities, using radically new tactics. Against the swords and shield-wall of the south, Philip threw a phalanx of pike-wielding infantry backed up by heavy cavalry.

Commanding the cavalry wing was his 18-year-old son, Alexander. Two years later, following Philip's assassination, he became king and began the meteoric career which made him a legend.

Alexander had been groomed in the warrior skills of Macedon and in the finer arts of civilised Greece, the philosopher Aristotle having been his tutor, but he is remembered above all as a brilliant general.

A year after his father's death, Alexander crushed a revolt by the Thebans and sacked their city, consolidating Macedon's control of the Greek mainland.

In 334BC he invaded Asia Minor, defeating a Persian army on the River Granikos, and six years later all Persia was his. Pushing east, he took Sogdiana (Uzbekistan), Bactria (Afghanistan) and reached India, but his exhausted soldiers

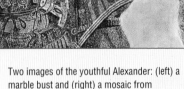

Two images of the youthful Alexander: (left) a marble bust and (right) a mosaic from Pompeii

refused to go further.

Returning to Persia in 324BC, he planned to forge Persia and Greece into one empire, but met strong opposition. Before he could overcome it, he died of fever. He was 33 years old.

His empire quickly collapsed as his generals set up kingdoms for themselves in the east, though Macedon remained the major power in Greece until Rome defeated its last independent king, Perseus, at Pydna in 167BC.

GETTING AWAY FROM IT ALL

It was a land of scintillating diversity,
a cornucopia of riches.
It was almost part of the mainland,
but not quite. It was an island,
but an island apart from the rest.
And it was only two hours from Athens.

SARA WHEELER
An Island Apart (1993)

Spetsai's tiny beaches and pretty houses are a stone's throw from the streets of Athens

ARGO-SARONIC ISLANDS

Frequent fast hydrofoils bring the beaches and pretty villages of these attractive islands close to Athens. Flying Dolphins/Ceres Hydrofoils provide services to and from the islands and their offices are situated at Akti Themistokleous 8, Freattys 185 36 Piraeus (tel: 4280 001). Journey times from Piraeus range from half an hour to 2 hours.

AÍYINA (Aegina)

The largest of the Argo-Saronic islands and the closest to Athens, Aegina is a favourite weekend resort of Athenians wanting peace and quiet. Visit Aegina to swim, eat at seafood tavernas, and visit the temple.

Naos Aphaia (Temple of Aphaia)

The Doric temple to Aphaia, protectress of women, retains most of its 32 columns.
On the hilltop close to the northeast tip of the island (tel: 0297 32398). Open: Monday to Friday, 8am–5pm; weekends, 8.30am–3pm. Admission charge. 40 minutes from Athens.

ANGÍSTRION

A tiny island with one little fishing-harbour-cum-resort, Angístrion seems much more remote than it is. Only a few hundred metres from Aegina, its beaches are usually much less crowded. Come here to do nothing except swim, sunbathe and relax.
30 minutes from Aíyina by boat.

Ídhra (Hydra)

Rows of whitewashed mansions rise above a port crowded with fancy yachts and cruisers as well as the inevitable fishing boats. There are no roads outside the village, but there are coves and pebbly beaches for swimming within walking distance of the village.
1 hour and 40 minutes from Athens.

Póros

A stone's throw from the mainland, the village is a multicoloured clutter of houses and the harbour bustles with hydrofoils and ferries. There are good beaches on the mainland opposite, and small boats shuttle to and fro every few minutes.
1 hour from Athens.

Spetsai

Spetsai sits at the mouth of the Argolikós Kólpos (Argolic Gulf) a short hop from the mainland. The village is an attractive mix of 18th-century shipowners' mansions and neo-classical 19th-century buildings, surrounding two harbours, the older fishing port and the newer harbour where ferries and hydrofoils dock. Much of the island is covered by pine woods and there are pleasant walks and good beaches. *2–2½hours and 30 minutes from Athens.*

ÉVVOIA (Evia)

Greece's second-largest island is only a couple of hours away from Athens via frequent ferry services from Rafína and Marmári and Káristos, a small resort near the south tip, which has an enormous pebble beach, a ruined Turkish castle, and lots of seaside tavernas. You can also get to Evia by car, as a swing bridge connects it to the mainland at Khalkís (Khalkidha) (see map on page 47).

LEVKÁS

This delightful Ionian island is connected to the mainland by a long causeway. There are beautiful white beaches on the west coast and an archipelago of uninhabited islands dotted around the sheltered waters of the east coast (see map on pages 98–9).

SKÍATHOS

The pine-covered island of Skíathos has some of Greece's finest sandy beaches, and its beautiful island capital with its Italianate clock towers and red-tiled houses is a package-holiday favourite. *Daily hydrofoil services from Vólos in summer.*

THÁSOS

Thásos is a huge, pine-covered island only an hour by the frequent ferry service from Kaválla. It has excellent sandy beaches.

Sunset over Póros. The coastline to the north is inaccessibly mountainous

Glossy ibis (*Plegadis falcinellus*) is one of the rarer birds in Greece

BIRDWATCHING

The rivers and wetlands of the Greek mainland offer some of the finest birdwatching in Europe.

AKHELÓÖS

The vast expanse of the Akhelóös delta is one of the finest birdwatching areas in Greece. The river reaches the sea through a maze of channels, among reedbeds, lagoons, cotton and maize fields and stands of eucalyptus. The shoreline is a marshy patchwork of lagoons, salt-pans and shallow, muddy bays. Kingfishers, larks and wagtails infest the river channels, and nearer the shoreline you can expect to see herons, egrets, many gull species, cormorants and terns.

About 30km from Mesolóngion (see page 94).

ANGELOKHORION

The salt-pans at Angelokhorion, near Thessaloníki, attract Mediterranean gulls, slender-billed gulls and Audouin's gull in spring and autumn, as well as many kinds of wader and tern. You may also spot Cory's shearwater flying close inshore.

Near Ayía Triás, southeast of Thessaloníki.

ÉVROS

The mud-flats and salt-marshes of the Évros delta attract waders of all kinds, herons, storks, pelicans, cormorants, plovers and larks.

About 30km east of Alexandhroupoli (see page 120).

LÍMNI MIKRÍ PRÉSPA (Lake Mikri Prespa National Park)

Pelicans, pygmy cormorants, egrets, ibises and storks haunt the reedbeds of the remote lake. Huge flocks of jays can often be seen in the beech woods surrounding the lake.

35km north of Kastoría (see page 129).

LÍMNI VISTONIS (Lake Vistonis)

Salt-pans and a lagoon lie south of the causeway which cuts Lake Vistonis in two, carrying the main road.

Another causeway leads to the island church of Ayios Nikolaos, which is an ideal vantage-point for spotting ibises, egrets, pygmy cormorants, pelicans and herons.

Midway between Xánthi and Komotiní (see page 120–1).

MESOLÓNGION

The lagoon at Mesolóngion with its fish hatcheries and salt-pans attracts curlews and many other waders, avocets, black-winged stilts, terns and gulls, and Kentish plovers.

(See page 94–5.).

NÉSTOS RIVER

Look out for herons, terns, gulls, waders

and (very rarely) flamingoes among the lagoons just north of Keramotí, close to the mouth of the Néstos river.
East of Kaválla. Follow signs to Gravouna, then Keramoti.

Right: Stork's nest on a telephone pole
Below: Long-nosed viper (*Vipera ammodytes*)

WILDLIFE

The wild mountains of Greece are home to some of Europe's last wolves and bears, though you are most unlikely to see them. Wolves are claimed to be on the increase in the northern mountains and are ruthlessly hunted, getting the blame for attacks on flocks which are more likely to be the work of dogs. Bears are rare and very shy.

The same hill country which shelters these vanishing predators is also the home of the spectacular griffon vulture and the lammergaier vulture, two of Europe's largest raptors, and of harriers, buzzards and golden eagles.

A variety of snakes, including vipers, smooth snakes and grass snakes, are common, and killed impartially whether venomous or not. Rocky hillsides and stone walls are the haunt of many species of lizard, including several species of wall lizard and the larger, more vivid green lizard and the distinctive eyed lizard. Geckos are found clinging to walls after dark and often gather around electric lights which attract the insects they feed on. Terrapins congregate in ponds and rivers, where they like to bask in sunny locations on banks and logs.

Land tortoises are found everywhere but are commonest in the Píndhos Óros (Píndhos mountains) and are all too frequently seen squashed on the road.

FLOWERS & BUTTERFLIES

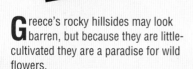

Greece's rocky hillsides may look barren, but because they are little-cultivated they are a paradise for wild flowers.

Much of the country is deemed suitable only for goat pasture, and wild flowers are left to flourish without interference.

In addition, Greek farming is still piecemeal, allowing wild plants to thrive in fields, orchards and olive groves alongside cultivated plants.

The best time to see Greece in bloom is in spring (as early as March in the southern Peloponnese or as late as June in the north) when hillsides and plains are ablaze with red, yellow and purple. Wild orchids are abundant, as are cistus, anemones, poppies, irises, gladioli, vetches, crocuses and many others. Purple and blue morning glories cover ruined walls, and every watercourse is marked by the pink flowers of oleander. Even after the lower regions have been scorched dry by the summer sun, the high slopes of Taïyetos and Píndhos where melting snow prolongs the spring may be a happy hunting ground.

Greece's climate and soil suit many species of orchid. As early as February you can hope to spot the giant orchids (*Barlia sp.*) and some varieties of bee orchid in the southern Peloponnese, and mountain-loving helleborine orchids may be found on north-facing slopes as late as July.

Unfortunately, European Union subsidies are encouraging many Greek

Far left: Hummingbird hawk moth
(*Macroglossum stellatarum*)
Left: the Scarce swallowtail butterfly
(*Iphiclides podalirius*)
Below: Giant orchid (*Barlia robertiana*)

farmers to experiment with more intensive cultivation. As a result, crops in parts of the mainland are becoming less varied, reducing the opportunities for wild flowers to flourish.

The range of food plants available and the limited use of insecticides make Greece a butterfly heaven, and the vivid colours of butterfly wings are all the more readily spotted against the greys and browns of dry summer landscapes.

Among the most exotic butterfly species are the huge, zebra-striped scarce swallowtail (*Iphiclides podalirius*), the southern swallowtail (*Papilio alexanor*), and the plain tiger (*Danaus chrysippus*). On hillsides, look out for the many different species of fast-flying fritillaries, and in fields and road verges watch for the flashing wings of more than a dozen species of blues.

The day-flying hummingbird hawk moth is a common denizen of flower gardens and fields, unmistakable because of its long, curling tongue and its ability to fly backwards with fast-beating wings. Its night-flying relatives, the huge poplar hawk moth, lime hawk moth and oleander hawk moth, are often drawn to unshaded lights after dark.

The Olympus trail zigzags steeply through pine woods and treeless peaks

CLIMBING ÓLIMBOS ÓROS (MOUNT OLYMPUS)

Greece's mightiest mountain has nine peaks of more than 2,600m. The highest, Mitikas, reaches 2,917m.

Allow three days and two nights for the climb. Enter Ólimbos National Park from the village of Litokhoron, near the foot of the mountain and drive, walk, hitch-hike or take a taxi to Prionia at 1,100m. From here a well-trodden trail zigzags steeply through pine woods to the Greek Alpine Club's Refuge A, a 3-hour hike. The refuge, at 2,100m, sleeps 90 people in bunk-bedded dormitories. Simple but filling meals are available.

Start for the summit immediately after breakfast, following a trail marked by metal arrows to Olympus's third-highest summit, Skala.

Do not attempt the final 200m separating Skala from Mitikas without an excellent head for heights and some climbing experience. On one side of the ridge between the two peaks there is a vertical, 500m drop. On the other, the path is no more than a series of holds.

Skolio, the mountain's second-highest peak, is an easy 750m walk from Skala. Allow 7 hours for the round trip from Refuge A to the summit and back.

Nights on Olympus are chilly and the days cool. The refuge provides blankets, but you should take a sweater and windproof jacket. Other essentials include a water-bottle, good boots, and dried fruit or chocolate.

Book accommodation in advance. Ellinikos Oreivatikos Syllogos Litokhoron (Greek Alpine Club of Litokhoron), Kentriki Platia, 60200 Litokhoron (tel: 0532 81944). Open: May to October, 8am–noon and 4pm–6pm. Katafigion A (Refuge A) (tel: 0352 81800). Open: May to October, 6am–10pm.

CRUISES

Among the most popular cruises are those taking in the delightful villages of the Kikhlades (Cyclades) islands. Cruises can be as short as one day or as long as a week, and can be arranged through any Athens travel agency or through major hotels.
Dolphin Hellas Cruises. *Akti Miaouli 71, 185 37 Piraeus (tel: 4512 109).*
Epirotiki Lines. *Akti Miaouli 87, 185 38 Piraeus (tel: 4291 000).*
Sun Line. *Iassonos 3, 185 37 Piraeus (tel: 4523 417).*

YACHTING

There are dozens of yacht charter companies in Greece, most of them based in and around Athens. Yachts can be chartered with or without a licensed crew. The weather is suitable for sailing from April to October, though in August the strong Meltemi wind can keep boats in harbour for up to three days at a time.
A list of yacht charter companies is available from the Greek National Tourist Office (see Directory, page 189).

DIRECTORY

To describe the Athenian
character in a word,
one might truly say that
they were born into the
world to take no rest
themselves and
to give none to others.

THUCYDIDES
Athenian general and historian
(460–400BC)

Shopping

*T*here are bargains to be found, especially in Athens. If you are shopping for distinctive regional products – such as rugs and blankets from Arákhova or silverware from Ioánnina you may find them cheaper in Athens than in the villages in which they are made.

Shops traditionally open between 8am and 1pm, close until around 5pm then reopen until about 8pm, though in Athens many souvenir shops stay open all day and late into the night. Most shops close on Sundays except in resort areas.

Antiquities and imitations
Genuine antiques and icons require an export permit (rarely granted), and in any case are very thin on the ground. Beware of fakes. The major archaeological museums licence a range of accurate and attractive replicas of

ancient statues, vases, jewellery and other finds, and these are a much better buy.

Beads and bangles
Brightly coloured ceramic beads, necklaces, gold and silver-plated bracelets, and the black and blue glass beads traditionally believed to ward off the evil eye make cheap and cheerful gifts. *Kombolói* or 'worry-beads', carried by many Greek men, are sold very cheaply in souvenir stores and at every street kiosk.

Clothing
Good buys include cotton sweaters. Thessaloníki, a centre of textile manufacturing, is the cheapest place in Europe for leading-brand denim jeans, shirts and jackets.

Flokati rugs
Huge, shaggy rugs of wool tufted on to a woven backing may be in natural, unbleached wool or dyed in a variety of vivid colours. Still widely used in Greek homes, they are sold throughout the country.

Footwear
Boots and shoes are well made and affordable. The best buys are to be found in main-street stores where Greeks shop.

Hand-made embroidery is a dying art and one of the best buys you can make

The sandals sold in tourist markets rarely wear well.

Herbs
Oregano, marjoram and thyme are among the better-known varieties, and prices are much lower than in your supermarket at home. Herbal teas are also widely sold in produce markets.

Jewellery
Jewellers abound, in smaller provincial capitals as well as in Athens, selling gold and silver jewellery based on ancient designs or on more modern interpretations. Prices reflect the value of the material, and while silverware may be cheaper than elsewhere in Europe, gold can be more expensive. Craftsmen in Ioánnina still make silver filigree work, sometimes decorated with turquoise. Antique silver buckles and belts can sometimes be found, but there is no guarantee of authenticity.

Leather goods
Leather handbags, satchels and travelling bags made solely for the tourist market are sold in markets everywhere. Prices are low and get lower with bargaining, but workmanship is not always first rate. Examine seams, straps and buckles before buying.

Museum shops
The official shops at major museums sell fine copies of ancient works. They cost little more than the poorer imitations sold in tourist shops, but are much better value.

Tax-free shopping
Value added tax at 18 per cent is charged on anything you buy. Tax-free shopping is available to visitors from outside the

Traditional worry-beads (*komboloi*) make cheap and cheerful souvenirs

European Union at selected shops in Athens and other major cities and resorts. A full list of shops offering VAT refunds to non-EU residents is available from: **Tax Free Club**, *Customer Service Office, Nikis 10, 105 63 Athens (tel: 3225 569 or 3240 802).*

Textiles and traditional handicrafts
Woven wool bags, blankets and rugs in bright colours and fine cotton embroidery and lace are among the best souvenirs you can buy. The National Welfare Association's handicraft programme, aimed at keeping Greek traditions alive, provides up to 5,000 women with equipment, designs and raw materials and sells their work through shops in Athens and elsewhere. *National Welfare Association, PO Box 1094, 10110 Athens (tel: 325 0524).*

The Kolonaki district offers the smartest shopping in Athens

SHOPPING IN ATHENS

Adhrianoú, which runs in a crescent through the Plaka, offers gift-hunters a rich choice of ceramics, T-shirts, scarves, hats, sweaters and leather goods made for the visiting shopper. Smart Athenians shop for clothes, shoes, jewellery and accessories elsewhere. The main downtown shopping areas are around Syntagma and Omonia, and in fashionable Kolonaki.

Similar types of store still tend to cluster together, oriental-style, on the same streets, so you will find a big choice of jewellers' stores on Voukourestiou and around the corner on Venizelou. There are more jewellers on Mitropoleos, which runs west from Syntagma and is also a good place to look for clothes, shoes and rugs.

BOOKS
Compendium
English-language books, magazines, travel guides and maps.
Nikis 28, Syntagma (tel: 3221 248).
Eleftheroudakis
Multilingual books, magazines, maps and guides.
Nikis 4 (tel: 3231 401), Sinopis 2 (tel: 7708 007), and Kifissias 294 (tel: 6878 350).

FLOKATI RUGS
Karamichos-Mazarakis Flokati
Handknotted rugs to new designs as well as traditional flokati.
Voulis 31–33 (tel: 3224 932).
Yannis Michalopoulos
Mnisikleous 8 (tel: 3240 384).

HANDICRAFTS
National Welfare Organization shops
sell handwoven rugs, embroidery, lace and other arts and crafts from all over Greece.
Voukourestiou 24, Ipatias 6 (inside the Hilton) and Vasilissis Sofias 46 (tel: 325 0524).

JEWELLERY
Athiniotakis
Voukourestiou 20 (tel: 3636 539).
Andreadis
Voukourestiou 24 (tel: 3608 544).
Lalaounis
Designs in gold and silver based on ancient motifs.
Panepistimiou 6 and Voukourestiou 12 (tel: 361 1371).
Zolotas
With Lalaounis, the best-known of the Athens gold and silver sellers.
Stadiou 19 (tel: 3240 871).

MUSEUM SHOPS
Mousio Benaki (Benaki Museum)
Greek handicrafts, textiles and jewellery. A good place to shop for gifts.
Koumbari 1 (tel: 361 1617).
Mousio Ethniko Arkheologiko (National Archaeological Museum)
Copies of many of the museum's finest exhibits.
Patission 28 (tel: 8217 717).
Mousio Goulandri Kykladhiki Texni (Goulandris Museum of Cycladic Art)
Accurate copies of the marvellous 5,000-year-old Cycladic figurines.
Neofytou Douka 4 (tel: 723 4931).

SHOES

Look for branches of the city-wide Mouger, Moschoutis or Petridis chains in main shopping areas.

MARKETS IN ATHENS

Ifaistou (Ifestou)

The original venerable Flea Market on Ifestou is a mixture of trendy clothes and shoe-stores, and glory-holes where you can buy anything from a postman's battered leather satchel to an army surplus parachute or a World War I artillery shell crafted into a beaten-brass flower vase. One long-established shop has a line in helmets which ranges from copies of those worn at the Battle of Marathón in 490BC to German and Italian headgear from World War II. Another sells antique prams, toys and carved animals from fairground carousels. The Flea Market is also a good place to buy hiking and camping gear. The best day to visit is Sunday, when the market spills over into surrounding streets and becomes a happy hunting ground for bargain-seeking Athenians.

Next to Monastiráki metro station.

Kendrikí Agorá (Central Market)

The Kendrikí Agorá (Central Market) is a photographer's heaven, though the squeamish may find the meat market section, with its racks of carcases and innards, a bit hard to take. The fish market, with stall after stall selling seafood from tiny whitebait to huge grouper and tunny, is spectacular. In surrounding streets are shops and stalls selling dried herbs and nuts, sweets, fruit, vegetables, game and household goods. The market cafés in the pre-dawn hours are a favourite rendezvous for Athenian nightlifers who have outlasted the city's bars and clubs. The market opens at first light.

10 minutes' walk from Monastiraki metro station, on the corner of Athinas and Evripidou.

Pandrosou (Pandhrossou)

Both sides of Pandhrossou are packed with shops selling smart leatherwear, fashion jewellery and replica antiques, and there is not a flea in sight. Most of the new shops take major credit cards.

You can find almost anything in the Plaka flea market

MARKETS AND SHOPPING AROUND GREECE

Away from Athens and the main holiday resorts, the stalls of the *laiki* (popular) market, where local people shop for fruit, vegetables and household supplies, are great places to shop and wander. The *laiki* is usually held several mornings a week in a main square or street. You can find out when and where at the local *dhimarkion* (town hall) or police station. Bargains include linen and embroidery, enamelled pots and pans, tiny coffee cups and – in recent years – Russian-made watches, cameras and binoculars peddled by Greek refugees from the former USSR. Village hardware stores, usually on or near the market square, are great places for souvenirs such as hammered brass and copper trays, goat-bells, striped blankets or walking sticks.

Several Greek towns have a special reputation for locally made products. Arákhova is known for its wool rugs,

Ioánnina for its silverware and Kastoría for its patchwork furs. Here and elsewhere, one shop is much the same as its neighbour and a walk down the main street will give you a good idea of what is for sale and how much it costs. Prices will be much of a muchness around town. Bargaining is common, but do not expect to beat the asking price down by more than about 10 per cent. Cash always commands lower prices than credit cards.

Arákhova

Coarsely-woven wool rugs and blankets dyed in earthy reds, orange and black are made locally and sold in stores along the main street, along with shepherds' twisty staffs and carved olive-wood kitchen ware.

Delphi

Modern Delphi's two main streets are packed with shops selling replicas from this and other archaeological excavations. Quality varies. The best bear the seal of approval of the National Archaeological Museum in Athens.

Ioánnina

A delightfully ramshackle bazaar area of medieval-looking workshops and stores lies just inland from Dionysou Filosofotou and the walled old town. For Ioánnina's famous silver filigree, visit the many jewellers' shops on Nissia, the island just offshore.

Kastoría

The lakeside city has been famous for its furriers for more than 2,000 years. Their speciality is piecing together garments

As elsewhere in the world the local market is the cheapest source of fresh produce

from scraps of fur, and most of their work can be bought as cheaply in Athens as from the workshops here. Beware, too, of buying garments made from the fur of endangered species. Though technically illegal, this trade continues to flourish. Buyers can be fined and their purchases confiscated by Customs on their return home.

Komotiní

An old-fashioned maze of streets northeast of Platia Ireni, the main square, houses a picturesque bazaar area and a bustling arcaded produce market. The antique shops along Venizelou, the pedestrianised main artery of the quarter, are piled with antique inlaid furniture, Turkish hookahs, lamps, vases and candlesticks – as well as with plenty of obvious fakes.

Olympia

Museum Art of Greece, *Leoforos Kondhíli (tel: 0624 22573)*, is outstanding not only for its fine replicas of statues and bronzes but also for its quality copies of Byzantine icons.

Thessaloníki

Thessaloníki's bazaar area – a rectangle bounded by Egnatias, Dhragoumi, Aristotelous and Tsimiski – offers the best street shopping in Greece. It is also a great place for photography, with stalls selling everything from live fish to fake designer watches. Look for these and other bargains on Venizelou and Ermou, or for colourful stalls selling fruit, vegetables, meat and seafood in the huge central market.

The **Thessaloníki Archaeological Museum** shop sells excellent replicas of exhibits and antiquities from this and other Greek museums.

Entertainment

*E*ntertainment in Greece embraces everything from the tragedies of Sophocles to the traditional music and dances of rural Greece, which are performed not only for tourists but for the Greeks' own enjoyment.

In Athens, several English-language newspapers and magazines (daily, weekly and monthly) have entertainment pages which list current performances. They include: *Athens News* (daily), *Athenscope* (weekly), *Athens Today* (monthly, free), *The Athenian* (monthly), *Greek News* (weekly). Elsewhere, your best bet is the local tourist office (see page 189), the *dhimarkion* (town hall) or, in holiday resorts, a travel and ticket agency.

CINEMAS

In major cities you can catch recently released US and European films with the original soundtrack and Greek subtitles. The video and television boom has forced many local cinemas in smaller towns to close.

Athens

Achilles, *Patission 140 (tel: 8656 355).*
Alexandra, *Patission 79 (tel: 821 9298).*
Athina, *Patission 122 (tel: 8233 149).*
Athinea, *Haritos 57, Kolonaki (tel: 7215 717).*
Atlantis, *Vouliagmenis 245 (tel: 9711 511).*
Attikon, *Platia Ay. Konstantinos (tel: 4175 897).*
Avana Assos Odeon, *Kifissias 234 (tel: 6715 905).*
Elly, *Akademias 64 (tel: 3632 798).*
Orphis, *Vouliagmenis 141 (tel: 9019 724).*
Palace, *Platia Pankratiou (tel: 7515 434).*
Plaza, *Kifissias 118 (tel: 6921 667).*

Thessaloníki

Alexandhros, *Ethnikis Aminis 1.*
Aristotelion, *Ethnikis Aminis 2.*
Esperos, *Svoulou 22.*
Makedhonikon, *Ethnikis Aminis/Filikis Eterias.*

CLASSICAL MUSIC

Classical music concerts take place frequently in Thessaloníki and Athens.

Athens

Athens Concert Hall, *Vasilissis Sofias, 11521 Athens (tel: 7225 511 and 7221 1169).*
Ethniki Lyriki Skini (National Lyric Theatre), *Akadimias and Charilaou Trikoupis (tel: 360 0180).*
Goethe Institut, *Omirou 14–16 (tel: 3608 111).*
Hellenic American Union, *Massalias 22 (tel: 3629 886).*
Pallas Theatre, *Voukourestiou 1 (tel: 3228 275).*

Thessaloníki

Kratiko Theatro, *Odhos Pavlou Mela/Platia Lefkou Pirgou (tel: 031 223785).*
Vasilio Theatro, *Odhos Pavlou Mela/Platia Lefkou Pirgou (tel: 031 261677).*

CULTURAL EVENTS

Several annual drama festivals aim to preserve Greece's ancient dramatic heritage side by side with modern productions and interpretations of the classical playwrights. Nobody with an interest in classical drama or in modern music, opera, ballet and dance should miss the simultaneous Athens and Epídhavros Festivals, held every year from mid-June to the end of September. The success of this twin event has encouraged the production of annual cultural festivals in other parts of Greece. Exact dates for each year are available from the Greek National Tourist Office (see **Practical Guide**, page 189).

Athens

For the annual **Athens Festival**, contact the Athens and Epídhavros Festival Box Office, Stadhiou 4 (tel: 3221 459/3223 111). Mid-June to late September.

Delphi

The **International Symposium on Ancient Greek Drama**, which includes theatre, music and dance performances and visual art exhibitions. June to August.
European Cultural Centre of Delphi (tel: 7233943).

Epídhavros

The annual **Epídhavros Festival**: performances of classical plays from the 5th century BC. Mid-June to mid-September. Held in the ancient Theatre of Epídhavros.
Epídhavros Festival Box Office (tel: 0752 22691).

Ioánnina

The **Ioánnina Festival**: classical and modern theatre and traditional dance. July to August.
The ancient theatre at Dhodhóni (tel: 0651 20090).

Shadow puppet. Sadly shadow plays are becoming increasingly rare in Greece

Kaválla

Festival of Philippi and **Thásos**: classical drama in the theatre at Filippi (Philippi) and on the island of Thásos. July to August *(tel: 051 223504).*

Thessaloníki

Dimitria Festival: classical and modern drama, music, ballet and opera performed by Greek and foreign companies.
October *(tel: 031 286519).*

MUSIC

Traditional Greek music is a mix of Eastern and Western influences. Greeks are fond of modern pop, but the wailing minor keys and unfamiliar rhythms of their own songs and dances have a strong flavour of the older, more oriental Greece. The most familiar music to visitors – played for the dance you are most likely to be invited to join – is the *sirtos*, a follow-my-leader circle-dance for any number of dancers. Typical instruments all over Greece include guitar, lute, fiddle and tambourine, with or without the accompaniment of various wind instruments typical of each region.

Bouzouki or *rembetika* music was brought to Athens by Greek refugees from Turkey in the 1920s and became fashionable among wealthy Athenians who would ostentatiously applaud the musicians by smashing their dinner-plates. The surviving *bouzouki* clubs of Athens are expensive and only for real enthusiasts. If you go, remember that smashing the crockery is an expensive kind of applause – you have to pay for the breakages.

Traditional ballads often recall the heroes of the epic struggle to throw off

wind instruments, including the *gaida*, a local version of the bagpipe, a shrill oboe called the *zournas*, and a type of flute called the *kaval*. Unlike the stately circles of Epirus, the regional dances are rapid and energetic, with much fancy footwork.

The typical folk music of the Peloponnese is the lively *palea dhimotika* ballad, driven along by guitar, fiddle and tambourine and recounting tales of daring, victory and defeat.

the Turkish yoke and many dances are re-enactments of historic incidents. In the north, these ballads include the mournful *kleftiko* of Epirus, celebrating the deeds of the *klefts*, mountain bandits who, like Robin Hood, are also remembered as heroes of the national resistance.

The music of Thrace and Macedonia features a number of unique

Greek bagpipes
(*gaida*)

DANCING

Dancing is a part of any celebration, even the most impromptu, for Greeks are still very much in the habit of making their own amusement.

Even among the fashionable youth of Greece, an evening spent dancing to the latest electronic beat may well end in the small hours with a traditional *sirtos*.

You can sample an evening of the kind of traditional entertainment Greeks enjoy at any *exoxiko kentro* (country centre). These are usually some kilometres from the nearest town, offering city-dwelling Greeks a nostalgic evening of home cooking, wine from the barrel, powerfully amplified traditional music, and dancing – both by performers and the audience.

One of the best places to sample Greek music and dance is at the **Dora Stratou Dance Centre**, *Théatro on Filopapou in Athens (tel: 3244 395)*. The late Dora Stratou was single-handedly responsible for saving much of Greece's musical heritage. She recorded many tunes and dances which had never been written down and were in danger of vanishing with the generation of villagers who remembered them. Her work rekindled interest in folk music, and the Dora Stratou troupes perform dances from all over the mainland and islands, not only at their own open-air theatre in Athens but at festivals throughout Greece and worldwide. The theatre is open nightly from May to September. Tickets are usually available on the night of the performance, or can be booked through agencies, main hotels, or from the theatre.

DISCOS

Tourism has combined with the Greek love of any kind of dancing to ensure that every holiday resort has an oversupply of discos and dance clubs. These start to warm up around midnight, play the latest dance hits at maximum volume and change name, ownership and venue virtually every season. Many are no more than an open-air dance floor, bar and sound system overlooking the beach. There is little to choose among them – pick whichever nightspot takes your fancy. Admission to clubs and discos is usually free, but drinks are more expensive than in an ordinary bar. Bigger indoor clubs with the usual lasers, dry ice and dance music can be found in Athens and Thessaloníki, but most of them close during the summer, when their DJs and many of their clientele head for the bright lights of the islands.

Athens
Absolut Dancing Club, *Filellinon 23 (tel: 3237 197)*.
Aerodhromio, *Pergamou 25*.
B-25, *Vouliagmenis 328*.

Greek women traditionally wore elaborately embroidered costumes and magnificent necklaces to dance on feast days and at weddings

Greek dancers in traditional costumes at the Dora Stratou Dance Centre

Thessaloníki

Barbarella, *Leoforos Mikras (1km from the airport – bus No. 78)*.

SOUND AND LIGHT

The Acropolis Sound and Light Show is viewed from seating on the Pnyx *(see page 37)*.

Tickets from Athens Festival box office (see below) or at the entrance on the Pnyx (tel: 9226 210). Operates daily, except Good Friday, April to October. Programmes: English, daily, 9pm–9.45pm; French, daily, except Tuesday and Friday, 10.10pm–10.55pm; German, Tuesday and Friday, 10pm–10.45pm.

TELEVISION AND VIDEO

The television is a fixture in every small rural *kafeneon* or taverna. The national TV channels ET1 and ET2 broadcast a steady diet of imported British and US films, programmes and soap operas which are subtitled in Greek. Satellite TV is spreading fast and is offered by most business hotels and many larger resort hotels. Many hotels and bars in the more popular international holiday resorts also offer a nightly programme of video movies, sports and music programmes from around the world. There is no charge for these – the idea is to lure you into the bar.

CAFÉ SOCIETY

The Greek café has undergone a quiet revolution in recent years. It is still the mainstay of local nightlife, but it is no longer restricted to older men. In most towns and villages the evening starts with the *volta*, a twilight stroll along the waterfront or around the *platia* by old and young – from wizened patriarchs and proud grannies showing off their latest grandchildren to dapper teenage dandies eyeing potential partners. Then the generations separate. Older women return home while their husbands settle down for an evening in a favourite old-style *kafeneon* to drink ouzo or coffee and talk politics over cards or backgammon. Meanwhile, the younger generation will hop from one bright new café-bar to the next. Bar-hopping can mean no more than moving to the next table – most cafés huddle together by the harbour or around the main square, and it takes an educated eye to figure out which outdoor tables belong to which bar. Owners of these glossy new establishments favour exotic names like Apocalypse, Bikini Red, Tequila Sunrise or No Name. An equally exotic selection of fancy imported liquor is always proudly on display behind the gleaming bar, but young Greeks are as likely to drink iced coffee – which is just as well, since the motorcycle is their favoured transport. And although the old *kafeneon* is traditionally an exclusively male domain, younger Greek women (like their boyfriends) head for the café-bars to see and be seen.

Café society: old and new

Festivals

The dates of many Greek festivals are set by the Orthodox calendar, and most of them celebrate one of the hundreds of Orthodox saints, some of them familiar in the West, some of them unique to the Orthodox Church. Many of the festivals are more or less private family affairs, with church services followed by a special meal served at home, but some are bigger and more public celebrations with parades, fireworks and public feasts in which the whole community may join. Because so many Greek village families have been separated by migration to the cities or overseas, the biggest and most emotional celebrations are those like the Assumption of the Virgin Mary (see below), when all the members of the scattered family return to their ancestral home.

1 January

Ayios Vassilios (St Basil), the Greek equivalent of Santa Claus, comes not on Christmas Day but New Year's Day.

6 January

Epiphany is mainly a religious festival when village wells, springs and the baptismal font of the village church are blessed. At some seaside locations young men traditionally dive for a blessed crucifix, but this custom is dying out.

Lent

The three-week period of Lent is marked by feasting, carnival and parades,

reaching a peak seven weeks before Easter (see pages 158–9). The biggest and noisiest celebrations are at Patras, where the carnival features a fancy-dress parade, dancing and music. There are celebrations and events too in Athens and Thessaloníki.

25 March

The Feast of the Annunciation is also celebrated as Independence Day (a bit prematurely as the date marks the beginning of the War of Independence in

Celebrating one of Greece's many Orthodox festivals

1821, not the eventual recovery of all the territories of modern Greece more than a century later).

23 April
Ayios Yioryios, the patron saint of shepherds, is honoured at village churches in the Píndhos mountains and elsewhere. One of the more accessible celebrations is at Arákhova, on the slopes of Parnassós.

April-May
Make your arrangements well in advance if you plan an Easter visit as all of Greece – and Greeks from all over the world – converge on their family's village and transport and accommodation are at a premium. Easter in Greece is celebrated according to the Orthodox calendar and can be up to three weeks ahead of or behind the Western Easter. Exact dates for Easter and other moveable feasts can be obtained each year from the Greek National Tourist Office (see **Practical Guide**, page 189).

1 May
May Day is both a traditional holiday on which people gather armfuls of brightly coloured wild flowers to make wreaths which hang above the door until midsummer, and a day of celebration and demonstration for Greece's strong left-wing parties.

18–19 July
Profitis Ilias (the Prophet Elijah) is honoured at his chapel on the highest peak of Taïyetos and at other mountain chapels.

15 August
Apokimisis tis Panayias

(Assumption of the Virgin) is second only to Easter in importance. Transport and accommodation can be hard to find, because Greeks return to the family village not only from the cities but from overseas. It is a great family celebration, with food, drink and dancing often until daybreak, and well-behaved visitors will be made welcome.

26 October
Ayios Dhimitrios, patron saint of Thessaloníki, is celebrated here and elsewhere with extensive sampling of the first of the summer wine.

28 October (Ochi Day)
Only the Greeks could celebrate as a national holiday their entry into a war which devastated their country, but celebrate it they do. It commemorates General Ioannis Metaxas's laconic negative response to the Italian ultimatum of 1940 – 'Ochi' (see page 110). Parades, music and dancing mark the event.

25 December
Christmas in Greece is not the major festival or commercial event that it is elsewhere. It is an important religious occasion and is marked by special church services, but there is little public celebration.

31 December
Children traditionally make the rounds of the village or neighbourhood singing carols, and adults get together with neighbours or family.

Traditional dress for Independence Day

EASTER

Easter in a Greek village is a never-to-be-forgotten experience. The biggest event of a crowded festival calendar, it combines solemn religious ceremony, emotional family reunions, and plenty of public song and dance. Most Greek festivals are first and foremost family affairs, celebrated in the home, but Easter spills out into village streets and cafés. With the weather often at its best, and everyone in a holiday mood, Easter is a great time to visit. Winter is over, and the busy summer season has not begun.

For Greeks living abroad, it is a time to go back to their roots. For their children, brought up in the USA, Canada or Australia, it may be the first taste of the very different lifestyle of a Greek village.

A far less commercial event than Christmas in English-speaking countries, Easter is impossible to avoid. The week's sacred events at cathedrals and churches throughout Greece are broadcast continuously on radio and television, and you will hear the solemn Gregorian chants of the Orthodox Church issuing from every place of worship. Bishops and priests abandon their everyday black for the gorgeous, gold-encrusted robes and jewelled crowns worn only for the most sacred occasions. In many places, ancient icons are carried in procession, and outside the churches the air is heavy with incense. Public worship begins on the evening of Good Friday and reaches a climax the following day with midnight mass, the lighting of thousands of candles to reaffirm the Resurrection, and an eruption of

fireworks. Easter Sunday traditionally begins with the breaking of the Lenten fast and a lamb or goat is roasted whole for Sunday lunch. Traditionally, red-dyed hard-boiled eggs are handed out as a special Easter delicacy. General merry-making with friends, family and neighbours continues through the day and late into the night. Village-wide hangovers on Monday morning are not uncommon.

Easter is a mixed time of sombre religious ceremonies and boisterous family gatherings
Far left: red-dyed eggs are a special Easter treat
Below: Easter cakes

Children

*G*reece welcomes children warmly and there are very few places anywhere where they cannot be taken. Couples will frequently be cross-examined as to whether or not they have children and if not, why not? Greeks regard children as an unmixed blessing, and crying babies or the fractious late-night behaviour of tired youngsters will be tolerated in village tavernas and cafés.

The National Gardens in Athens offer an escape from the city traffic for children and parents

Food

Food should not be a problem, even if your children are picky eaters who insist on a chips-only diet. These are on every Greek menu, as are other plain and familiar dishes such as fish, burgers, and salad. Canned soft drinks are universally available, as are most well-known brands of sweets and chocolate bars, ice-cream and ice lollies. Sticky Greek cakes and desserts from the *zacharoplasteion* (pastry shop) are also a hit with young children. Greece is above all a country where life is lived outdoors almost all year round, and Greek youngsters are raised on a free-range basis with the whole village and its surroundings as a playground. Visiting toddlers can easily join in.

The seaside

The main attraction for families visiting Greece is the beach, and sea and sand are the focus of most family resorts. Greece's seas have little or no tide, so the sea is always at your doorstep and is almost always calm enough even for young children to swim in safety. Sheltered, gently-shelving sandy beaches ideal for families with small children can be found on the Khalkidhiki (Chalkidiki) peninsulas in Macedonia (see pages 122–3), in the southern Peloponnese at Koróni and Methóni (see pages 64–5) and Stoupa (see page 77), and in Argolis at Tolón (see page 58).

Things to do

Children with an interest in wild flowers and wildlife will find Greece a delight, with dozens of birds, lizards, tortoises and turtles, butterflies and other insects to identify and watch. Those with an interest in marine life will find the clear waters of inlets and harbours as full of sea creatures as any marine aquarium, and will be fascinated by the varied haul unloaded by fishing boats each morning. The end of any Greek village pier always attracts a gaggle of junior anglers, and simple hook-and-line kits are sold in all village shops.

Pedaloes, canoes, and other simple watersports equipment are for hire at all summer beach resorts, and older children can use them with confidence in

Greek youngsters have the run of the village and the taverna

shallow waters and enclosed coves. Although Greek waters have virtually no tides, they do have inshore currents so caution must be used. Bicycles for children and adults can also be rented at some resorts.

Children with an interest in history will find that the ancient sites, medieval castles and deserted fortresses of mainland Greece offer a fascinating 'hands-on' lesson in the past, and younger children will enjoy scrambling to the highest tiers of the ancient theatres. Running races in the millennia-old stadium at Olympia or Delphi can be a welcome release of energy after the journey. In the unlikely event of poor weather, a visit to one of the many folklore museums with their displays of traditional costumes, kitchenware, tools, weapons and jewellery will keep children entertained.

Purpose-built facilities and entertainment for children are rarely provided. Most villages have a small playground, though old-fashioned wood and metal swings and roundabouts are potential hazards for smaller children. Some larger resorts and hotels have separate swimming pools for toddlers, and many package tour operators offer fun-clubs, child-minding and babysitting services (see **Practical Guide**, page 181).

Sandy Greek beaches offer children hours of pleasure

Sport

*T*he great sporting passions of Greece are basketball and soccer, which are watched avidly both live and on television and are enthusiastically played at all levels. It is a small village indeed which does not have a dusty football pitch on its outskirts and a basketball pitch in its schoolyard or outside the village hall.

Basketball has become a national passion, rivalling football

Basketball has outstripped soccer in the popularity stakes, partly because the national team performs strongly in international events, but the Greek soccer team's success in qualifying for the 1994 World Cup in the USA helped to rekindle enthusiasm for soccer. You will see graffiti acclaiming the top Athenian team, Panathinaikos (PAO), not only all over Athens but all over the country.

BASKETBALL
Greek Basketball Federation,
N Saripolou 11, Athens (tel: 8244 125).

SOCCER
Matches are played regularly on Sundays at 5.30pm in season (October to April) and tickets are available at each team office.
Greek Soccer Federation, *Syngrou 137, Athens (tel: 9336 410).*
The most important national venue for football and other sporting events is the Peace and Friendship Stadium, *Nea Faliron, Athens (tel: 4819 513).*

SPORTS FOR VISITORS

GOLF
Greece has the ideal climate for golf, especially in spring and autumn, but there are only two courses on the mainland which approach international standards.
Glyfadha Golf Club
The only high-quality golf course in Greece is in the seaside suburb of Glifádha (Glyfadha), with an 18-hole course, dressing rooms, sports store, restaurant and bar. *12km from central Athens, signposted (tel: 8946 820).*
Porto Carras
The Porto Carras resort complex, Khalkidhikí *(tel: 0375 71221).*

RUNNING
The heroic first Marathon run (see page 50) is re-enacted twice a year, for seeded athletes in April and for all runners in October. Details from **SEGAS** (Greek

Sports and Athletics Federation), *Syngrou 137, Athens (tel: 9359 302).*

SKIING

Skiing is increasingly popular in Greece, and although Greek slopes do not rank with the best in Europe they are certainly among the cheapest. The ski season begins in mid-December and continues until the end of April, when you can combine a day's skiing with a holiday on the beach or touring. The main ski centres are at Parnassós, near Delphi (see page 86 and 96–7) and on Pelion (see pages 112–13).

Parnassós Ski Centre
24km from Arákhova (tel: 0234 22689).
Pelion Ski Centre
27km from Vólos (tel: 0421 25696).

TENNIS

There are tennis courts on a number of the beaches managed by the Greek National Tourist Office and at many major resorts. For further information, contact **EFOA** (Greek Tennis Association), *Omirou 8, Athens (tel: 3230 412)* or the **Athens Tennis Club**, *Vasilissis Olgas, Athens (tel: 9232 872).*

YACHTING

Yachts of all sizes are available for charter from Greek marinas, with or without skipper and crew. With hundreds of coves and beaches accessible only by sea, uninhabited offshore islets and hideaway harbours, Greece is the best yachting country in the Mediterranean. A list of yacht charterers is available from the Greek National Tourist Office (see page 189).

Hellenic Sailing Federation, *Akti Navarchou Kountouioti, Kastella, Piraeus (tel: 4137 531).*
Yacht Club of Athens, *Karageorgis Servias, Mikrolimano, Piraeus (tel: 4127 757).*
Naval Club of Thessaloníki, *Themistokli Sofouli 112 (tel: 031 414521).*
Porto Carras Naval Club, *Neos Marmaras, Sithonia (Sidhonia), Khalkidhikí (tel: 0375 71381).*

Ski season on Mount Parnassós lasts from December until early April

Greek waters provide perfect conditions for windsurfing

WATERSKIING

Waterskiing facilities are available at all holiday beaches in summer and there are waterski schools at most major resorts. For further information, contact the **Greek Waterskiing Association**, *Stournara 32, Athens (tel: 5231 875)*.

WINDSURFING

Greece's waters, with their reliable breezes, are perfect for windsurfing and boards are for hire at every beach resort. A number of international events are held each year. For details, contact the **Greek Windsurfing Association**, *Filellinon 7, Athens (tel: 3230 068)*.

ADVENTURE SPORTS

Greece's mountain landscapes are an adventure playground offering an exciting and extensive range of activities above and below ground, in the air and on the water.

CAVING

The limestone rock of mainland Greece is riddled with long cave systems and underground lakes and rivers. Many of these have been opened up to visitors under the management of the Greek National Tourist Office, but kilometres of caverns still remain to be explored. **Hellenic Speleological Society**, *Mantzarou 8, Athens (tel: 3617 824)*.

CLIMBING AND TREKKING

Greece's mountains are wonderful for walkers, offering relatively gentle routes which can be completed in one or two days as well as much more demanding itineraries. Mount Olympus, the highest mountain in Greece and the second highest in the Balkan region, is a surprisingly undemanding ascent and from May to mid-October is within the abilities of most reasonably fit walkers, with well-marked trails and dormitory accommodation in several mountain refuges. Allow three days for the ascent and descent, with two nights' stay in a mountain refuge (see page 140). Another relatively easy trek, which can be completed in one day, takes you to Drakolimin, a mountain lake on the slopes of Tímfi Óros (Mount Timfi) in the Píndhos range (see pages 110–1). In the same region, the spectacular Vikos Gorge offers a demanding one- or two-day hike for fitter walkers. In southern Greece, the ascent to Profítis Ilías, the highest peak of the Taïyetos range, is still more demanding. The Greek Alpine Club, which manages refuges on all these mountains, publishes a range of guides and detailed route maps and can advise on mountain conditions, equipment and when to go.

Rock climbing is growing in popularity, but the soft, crumbly limestone of most Greek mountains is not ideal climbing rock, attractive though it looks.

Basic mountain safety rules must be obeyed even on shorter walks, as the mountains are thinly populated and a sprained ankle far from help can spell disaster. Take plenty of water, and make sure that someone knows where you are going and when you expect to be back. Nights on the higher slopes are chilly even in high summer, and you will need proper walking boots – not just trainers – for more serious trekking. Other essentials include a water-bottle and water sterilising tablets.

EOS (Greek Alpine Club) maintains refuges with dormitories on the main trekking routes. On Olympus, these are staffed and serve simple meals. Elsewhere, they are usually unstaffed and you must get the key from the local EOS office in the nearest village. The EOS also supplies information, bulletins and maps.

Ellinikos Orivatikos Sindhesmos (EOS), *Karageorgis Servias 7, Athens (tel: 3234 555).*

HANG-GLIDING

The bright-coloured delta wings of hang-gliders can often be seen circling over the steep ridges of the Píndhos mountains near Ioánnina (page 104–5) which create great up-draughts.

Delta Wing Gliding School, *Apollo 44, Piraeus, Athens (tel: 5247 516).*

SCUBA DIVING

Until recently the Greek authorities have held diving in deep suspicion, fearing the theft of antiquities from seabed sites. Key

underwater archaeological sites have now been thoroughly mapped and remain off-limits, but you can learn to dive at Vouliagméni and at Várkiza, near Athens (see page 49) and there is more extensive diving off the coast of Sidhonia (see pages 122–3). Rules for divers are strict and include a ban on touching, removing or even photographing any antiquities you find and on spear-fishing with scuba gear. Visibility in Greek waters is usually excellent, but there is less underwater life than you might expect – the result of thousands of years of intensive fishing.

Hellenic Federation of Underwater Activities, *West Airport Terminal Post Office, 16604 Ellenikon, Athens (tel: 9819 961).*

A rock climber pits his skill against the pinnacles and precipices of the Metéora

Food and Drink

WHAT'S ON THE MENU?

The best Greek food is the simplest: fish straight from the boat, vegetables fresh from the field served as salad with wild herbs and olives or in stews. Most restaurants offer multilingual menus. The translations can be as opaque as the original Greek, inviting you to sample 'smashed bowels in roasted spit' or 'one brain salad'. Puzzling them out is half the fun ('one brain salad' is just that – a sheep's brain served cold atop a bed of lettuce). You will sometimes be invited into the kitchen to choose your meal, while in the smallest restaurants you just take pot luck or make do with omelettes, chips and salad. Only in the smartest restaurants will food be served course by course.

Meze, a selection of dishes served simultaneously, is a Greek culinary tradition, and in smaller restaurants everything often comes at once or in an unexpected order – chips, for example, often arrive first as a kind of appetiser.

Fish

Fish is priced according to weight and category. You choose your fish from the kitchen, where it is then weighed and the price calculated before filleting. Seafood is popular but pricey, with delicacies like *barbounia* (red mullet) and *melanouryia* (no translation) at the top of the price range. Swordfish (*xifias*) steaks are always available and moderately priced, usually coming in enormous portions. At the cheaper end of the scale are *marides* (whitebait), *goupes* (sprats) and *kalamares* (fried baby squid). *Astakos* (langouste, though usually translated as lobster) is expensive by local standards, though most visitors will think it good value. Unfamiliar seafood dishes include *oktapodhi* (octopus) served in a variety of ways, either cold as a snack, grilled, or in a stew with rice or pasta.

In northern Greece, with its many lakes, you will find freshwater fish like carp and eel on the menu along with crayfish, lake crabs and frogs' legs.

Fresh fish is always on the menu in Greek harbour towns and holiday resorts

Octopus is a Greek favourite but an acquired taste for visitors

Meat dishes

Moussaka (lamb or veal cooked in layers of cheese and aubergine), *yiouvetsi* (beef stewed with noodles in a clay pot), *kotopoulo* (roast or grilled chicken) and *souvlaki* (veal, lamb or pork cooked on a skewer) appears on most menus. In the north, a spicy sausage called *spetsofai* is often served in a stew with vegetables. More familiar meat dishes include grilled lamb chops or pork cutlets, and *keftedhes* (meat balls in sauce). Chips are the favoured accompaniment to meat dishes.

Vegetable dishes

The 'traditional' Greek salad is a meal in itself, featuring heaps of tomatoes, onion, cucumber, green peppers, and olives drowned in oil and flavoured with dried herbs. It is known as *horiatiki* only in tourist restaurants, where it is usually served crowned with feta cheese (if you don't want cheese, ask for *salata hores feta*, salad without cheese).

Dishes like *gemista* (tomatoes or green peppers stuffed with herb-flavoured rice) and *dolmades* (stuffed vine leaves) may or may not contain meat. Vegetable-only dishes include *vriam* (ratatouille), and a variety of pulses including *fakes* (lentil stew), *gigantes* (stewed broad beans), *mavromati* (boiled black-eye beans served cold with coriander) and *fasolakia* (green beans stewed with tomatoes). Cold dishes include *tsatsiki* (yoghurt flavoured with cucumber and garlic).

A slab of strong-flavoured feta cheese is the heart of a hearty Greek salad

Stuffed tomatoes and peppers are a village staple and a treat for vegetarians

Meze snacks traditionally accompany a mid-morning glass of aniseed-flavoured ouzo

PLACES TO EAT AND DRINK

Greeks eat late, and dinner is the big meal of the day. In resorts where tourists outnumber locals, restaurants have adjusted to the foreign habit of eating early in the evening. If your first choice of restaurant is full, you will almost always find others, just as good, next door or near by. Dress codes are virtually non-existent for both men and women; generally, a clean shirt for men and anything other than beachwear for women is acceptable anywhere and most outdoor resort restaurants are accustomed to serving daytime clients in bathing suits.

Greek eating-places fall into a number of categories. Virtually all serve alcohol at all times (except on election day) but some offer a full menu, others only snacks, pot luck, or specialities. Most restaurants stay open late – Greeks set on a night out will dine at 10pm, stay till after midnight, then go on to a bar or nightclub. In summer,

Rizokalo (rice pudding flavoured with cinnamon)

almost all dining is al fresco, except in major cities.

Bar

Places described as bars or 'pubs' are usually smart, shiny and relatively expensive, serving cocktails and imported liquors and beers to a younger clientele and often open only after dark. In busier resorts, an early-evening 'happy hour' often attracts a noisy clientele. Bars usually serve only soft drinks, alcohol and iced coffee.

Estiatorion (Restaurant)

Open for lunch and dinner, the *estiatorion* is where Greeks go on family occasions. In major cities, restaurants can be quite formal but in resorts they are usually friendly and relaxed and offer the widest choice of meals and drinks.

Kafeneon

The *kafeneon* is the nearest thing Greece has to a neighbourhood bar or pub. Open all day and usually past midnight, it serves coffee (Greek or instant), Greek spirits, beer and *retsina*, often with a plateful of snacks such as sunflower seeds, cubes of cheese, or slices of sausage. It is a centre of village social life (or in big cities the focus for a block of shops or apartments) and many older men spend much of their day at a café table over tiny cups of coffee or glasses of *ouzo*.

Baklava from the corner pastry shop is only for those with a really sweet tooth

Ouzeri

The *ouzeri* serves *ouzo* (of course), wine, beer and coffee, almost always accompanied by *meze*, a series of substantial snacks which can add up to a light meal.

Psarotaverna (Fish Restaurant)

The *psarotaverna* specialises in seafood, usually overlooks the harbour, and is probably the most expensive place to eat. The menu will include the full gamut of fish and crustaceans, but few alternatives.

Psistaria (Grill Restaurant)

For carnivores only, the psistaria serves grilled meat of all kinds. The grill is usually up front, and like the *psarotaverna*, few alternative dishes are offered.

Taverna

A catch-all term for an unpretentious restaurant where you eat what is in the pot that day, washing it down with jugs of wine, the *taverna* is to be approached with caution. In out of the way corners of Athens and Thessaloníki there are delightful old tavernas where you can eat the best meal of your Greek holiday at a very affordable price. In busy holiday centres, however, anywhere calling itself a taverna is likely to be a tourist trap pure and simple. As a general rule, if most of your fellow diners are Greeks you are in for a treat; if they are foreigners, think twice.

Zacharoplasteion (Pastry Shop)

If you have a sweet tooth the *zacharoplasteion* is the place for you. Selling sweet pastries and sticky cakes to take away or eat at pavement tables, it also serves Greek and instant coffee and soft drinks.

Local diners at an old-style taverna in the city of Thessaloníki

Inside an old-fashioned restaurant on Monastiraki

RESTAURANTS

You can eat well in even the smallest of Greek villages. Most of them have more than their fair share of cheap and simple tavernas. In most resorts and country towns there is little to choose between one eating-place and its neighbour, so stroll along the harbour or round the square and pick whichever takes your fancy. Eat where the Greeks eat and you will find the food better, cheaper and more varied than in restaurants catering only to holidaymakers. Few restaurants in Greece are worth a special visit, and those as much for the view or the atmosphere as for the food. We have listed restaurants in Greece's three main cities, as well as a handful of other places which stand out from the crowd.

The following table is an indication of restaurant prices. The D (for drachma) sign indicates the cost of a three-course meal for one without wine. A half-litre carafe of *retsina* or beer costs around 350 drachmas, a bottle of red or white wine between 1,500 and 2,000 drachmas. Only the most up-market city restaurants accept telephone reservations (or even have a telephone). Prices may increase in drachma terms by up to 20 per cent a year, so only a rough price guide can be given.

D	under	DR3,000
DD	under	DR4,500
DDD	under	DR6,000
DDDD	over	DR6,000

ATHENS
Apotsos DD
This long-established *ouzeri* hidden in an arcade off Venizelou (Panepistimiou) is decorated with antique posters and is a lunchtime favourite with Athenians.
Venizelou (Panepistimiou) 10.

Bakalarakia D
The Athenian version of a fish and chip restaurant. Specialities include battered cod and *skordalia*, a dish made with mashed potatoes and garlic.
Kidhathineon 41.

Eden DD
The best vegetarian restaurant in Athens, with meatless moussaka as well as many traditional meat-free dishes. Closed Tuesday.
Flessa 3 (tel: 3248 858).

Fish restaurants DDDD
The small fishing harbour of Mikrolimano is surrounded by the best (and most expensive) fish restaurants in Athens.
Take a taxi (about 10–15 minutes from the city centre) or take the metro to Nea Faliron.

Gerofinikas DDDD
Grand, old-fashioned restaurant specialising in game and in rich Eastern-influenced dishes. Booking advisable.
Pindharou 10 (tel: 3636 710/3622 719).

O Platanos DDD
An outdoor grill-restaurant beneath an enormous plane tree. *Closed Sunday. Dioyenous 4.*

Taverna Dhimokritous DDD
The menu at this attractive restaurant in a lovely neo-classical building is more extensive than most.
Dhimokritou 23 and Tsakalof.

Theophilous DDD
This venerable taverna, decorated with frescos, opened in 1899. In the heart of the Plaka.
Vakhou 1 (tel: 3223 901).

IOÁNNINA
Nissi
Choose from a score of outdoor establishments serving freshwater fish and shellfish on Ioánnina's restaurant island. Most are on Monaxon Nektario-Theofanos, a small, tree-shaded *platia.*

MONEMVASÍA
To Kanoni DDD
Elegant restaurant in a restored 17th-century mansion, overlooking the roofs of the fortified medieval town.
Kastro (tel: 0732 61387).

PATRAS
Evangelatos DDD
Situated near the waterfront with views out to sea.
Ayiou Nikolaou 7 (tel: 277772).

Ippopotamos DDD
Up-market restaurant on Patras's pleasantly old-fashioned central square.
Platia Yioryiou 1 (tel: 270095).

Athens has elegant traditional restaurants as well as cheerful tavernas

Psari DD
Simple fish and grill taverna.
Ayiou Dhimitriou 75.

STOUPA
To Fanari DDD
On the headland just west of Stoupa, the restaurant has mind-blowing views back across the Messinian Gulf.

THESSALONÍKI
Krikelas DDD
The city's grandest and busiest taverna.
Gramou Vitsi 32 (tel: 414690).

Limaniotis DDD
An atmospheric seafood restaurant with live music in the evening. Near the harbour.
Navarhou Votsi 1–3.

Olymbos Naoussa DDD
Lunch-time restaurant with specialities including *midia tiganita* (fried mussels), elegant surroundings and a view of the sea. On the waterfront.
Nikis 5 (tel: 275715).

Stratis DDDD
A very popular restaurant with outstanding seafood. Reservations recommended.
Nikis 19 (tel: 234782).

Ouzo comes under many labels, but it always tastes of aniseed

BEVERAGES

Beer

Almost all the beers sold in Greece are
strong lagers, brewed locally under
licence and always served ice-cold.
Common brands include Amstel,
Henninger, Heineken, Kaiser and
Kronenburg, all around 5 per cent
alcohol by volume and usually sold in
550ml bottles. Imported beers such as
Beck's are often sold in smarter bars, and
brands such as Guinness and Newcastle
Brown Ale may be found in some resorts.

Prices vary widely and depend not so
much on what you drink as where you
drink it. A small bottle of imported beer in
a neon-lit cocktail bar may cost three times
as much as a large bottle in a local tavern.

Brandy

Locally made brandy – sometimes
described as *koniak* (cognac) – comes in
three-, five- and seven-star quality.
Sweeter than French brandies, it makes a
pleasant after-dinner drink. The best
known brands include Cambas and
Metaxa.

Coffee and tea

Kafes elliniko (Greek coffee) comes black and thick, in thimble-sized cups, and is always served with a glass of water. If you like it without sugar ask for *sketo*; if you like extra sugar ask for *glikou*. Most Greeks drink it *metrio*, with one measure of sugar. Instant coffee is universally known as Nes. If you want it hot ask for Nes *zesto* or you may be given *frappe* – iced instant coffee. *Tsai* (tea) is available almost everywhere and is invariably made with British Lipton's tea-bags. If you like your tea or coffee with milk, ask for it *me gála*.

Imported and local spirits

Imported liquors such as Scotch, bourbon, vodka and gin generally cost considerably more than the locally made versions, most of which are destined to be cocktail ingredients. Measures, however, are always generous.

Ouzo

Sunset is the customary time to take your Greek aperitif, though *ouzo* can be (and is) drunk at any hour of the day or night. A clear, sweet, aniseed-based spirit, it is always served with a glass of water and usually with ice. It turns cloudy when water is added.

Retsina

Retsina or 'resinated' wine was formerly stored in earthenware jugs proofed with pine resin, which gave it a distinctive flavour. Today, resin is added artificially. It is an acquired taste, but one worth acquiring, and is by far the cheapest of Greek wines when sold in 550ml bottles. In many villages the taverna will sell retsina *apo to bareli* (from the barrel) by the carafe and this is always well worth sampling.

Soft drinks

All the well-known soft-drink brands are available throughout Greece. Although Greek farmers dump surplus oranges by the roadside, freshly-squeezed orange juice (*ximo portokaliou*), available in most holiday resorts, is remarkably expensive.

Tsipouro

A clear and lethal spirit made (like Italian *grappa*) from the skins and pulp left over after pressing grapes to make wine, *tsipouro* is sold in miniature bottles in village tavernas all over the northern mainland.

Wine

Greece makes a range of red, white and dessert wines, all of them affordable and none of them outstanding. In general, white wine (*krasi aspro*) is a better bet than red wine (*krasi mavro*). Boutari, Cambas and Tsantali whites and reds are acceptable. Several small boutique wineries, including Hatzimihali and Lazaridhi, make better and more expensive wines, and are worth sampling if you can find them. Wines maybe categorised as either *ksero* (dry) or *glyko* (sweet).

Greek wines vary, but some of the best come from barrels like these

Hotels and Accommodation

*F*inding somewhere to stay is almost never a problem in Greece. There is accommodation to suit all pockets in all but the very smallest villages, and even in these you may find the local shopkeeper is willing to rent a spare room (or, in summer, a camp bed in the garden or on the roof). Bear in mind, though, that almost all pensions and hotels in summer holiday resorts close in mid-October and do not re-open until April. You will also find it tricky finding accommodation at Easter (see pages 158–9) and Apokimisis (see page 157) when millions of Greeks return to their ancestral villages. Book well ahead for these dates.

In theory, Greek accommodation is strictly controlled and licensed by the government. The reality is rather different. Nobody knows exactly how many rooms are available for rent each summer, as local entrepreneurs are continually adding more rooms and apartments, and in practice prices are determined not by the authorities but by market forces. If you turn up before or after the main holiday season you will find hoteliers much more willing to negotiate than in mid-summer. Most accommodation renters will take 10 per cent off the standard rate if you stay for three or more nights.

Accommodation is easy to find. Older hotels, built just before or after World War II, usually cluster around the main square of provincial towns or, in harbour towns, along the waterfront. In smaller villages and resorts, look out for signs offering rooms in privately run accommodation. These usually read 'Rent Rooms' or (for German visitors) *'Zimmer Frei'*. Until the 1980s, such accommodation was usually in the spare bedroom of a family home. These days, it is more likely to be in a purpose-built block with solar-heated hot water and en suite or shared shower and toilet.

In seaside resorts much of the holiday accommodation is in bright, newly built apartments with fully equipped kitchens. These are booked up by holiday companies in high season, but are often available at very reasonable rates in spring and autumn and are excellent value if you plan to stay in one place for a while.

Gythion Hotel, Yithion

Poolside at the Athens Hilton

All licensed accommodation is divided into categories A to E, with separate listings for hotels and for pensions and apartments. Rooms are rated not on quality but on the facilities available (a scruffy old-fashioned hotel with telephones and television in the rooms and a mediocre restaurant will be rated higher than a bright new one without such services). Hotels and pensions are also being built faster than they can be inspected and listed, so many attractive new properties have no rating. The system should be treated with caution. Most accommodation is on a room-only basis, and where breakfast is offered it is rarely worth the DR900–1,200 you pay.

Prices vary considerably depending on the season, and can increase by up to 20–30 per cent a year. When this book was researched a twin room with en suite facilities cost from around DR4,500 in a small family-run pension to DR45,000 in a top Athens hotel. A C-class hotel (equivalent to 3-star) cost between DR10,000 and DR15,000. D- and E-class hotels, many of them built between the wars, are usually very cheap and central but shabby and run-down. Few visitors will want to use them.

Most accommodation in seaside resorts closes between the end of October and the beginning of April.

❖

THOMAS COOK
Traveller's Tip

Travellers who purchase their travel tickets from a Thomas Cook network location are entitled to use the services of any other Thomas Cook network location, free of charge, to make hotel reservations.

Hotel Malvasía, Kastro, Monemvasía

APARTMENTS

Self-catering apartments are available in many holiday resorts, either as part of a package holiday or (in spring and autumn) for independent travellers. They usually have two bedrooms, with a lounge area which can be converted into a third bedroom, and a kitchen equipped with two-ring electric cooker, fridge, pots, pans, glasses, crockery and cutlery.

CAMPSITES

Campsites can be excellent value, especially if you are touring by car. They offer secure parking and camping spaces usually shaded by poplar and plane trees, and facilities usually include a simple restaurant, mini-market, communal showers with constant hot water, and a laundry area. Most campsites are on the coast, next to some of the best beaches in Greece, but there are also sites at places like Olympia and Delphi, many of them

with swimming pools. Prices are comparable with the cheapest rooms. Sites to be avoided include those in the Athens area, most of which are unkempt and ill equipped.

A list of campsites in Greece is available from the Greek National Tourist Office.

HOTELS

Hotels are classified from A to E, with most A-class properties in the Athens region. C-class hotels, the largest category, are found at all resorts and tend to be big, bland and busy in high season, echoing and empty the rest of the year. D- and E-class hotels, found in larger towns, are cheap but usually grubby and run-down.

PENSIONS

Small, family-run pensions, usually with around a dozen twin-bedded rooms, offer some of the best-value accommodation in Greece, especially off-season. Most of them are recently built, offering rooms with en suite facilities. Solar heating is universal, so do not expect hot water too soon after sunrise.

STAYING IN STYLE

The only international-name luxury hotels in mainland Greece are in Athens, most of them on Platia Syntagma in the city centre or on Leoforos Syngrou. Most have open-air pools as well as business centres, room service, and a choice of expensive restaurants and bars.

TRADITIONAL SETTLEMENTS

The Greek National Tourist Office operates a Traditional Settlements programme which aims to breathe new life into dying communities and to preserve some of the best of Greek vernacular architecture by converting traditionally built homes into comfortable guest-houses, installing modern facilities without changing the style of the building. These are not cheap (rates compare with B- and C-class hotels) but are worth every penny for their atmosphere and location among some of the most spectacular landscapes and most picturesque villages in Greece. There are traditional settlements in the Mani and in Monemvasía in southern Greece, in several of the villages of the Pelion peninsula in Thessaly, and in the Zagória villages in Epirus.

Most provide room-only accommodation. Reservations are essential. Further information from the Greek National Tourist Office (see page 189).

VILLAGE ROOMS

In some villages, old-style 'village rooms'

are still rented in family homes, where the beds are likely to be elderly and the price may seem disproportionately high. To balance this, you will get a glimpse of local life and as many cups of Greek coffee as you are willing to drink.

VILLAS

Luxury villas, some with their own pool and landscaped grounds, are available at some up-market resorts such as Vouliagméni on the outskirts of Athens, and are easiest to find as part of a package holiday. Most travel agents should be aware of tour operators offering villa packages.

YOUTH HOSTELS

Old-fashioned, crowded, dirty and usually burdened with tyrannical rules and regulations, Greek youth hostels are no cheaper than many privately-rented rooms or older D- and E-class hotels. Many so-called 'youth hostels', especially in Athens, are privately run and have no connection with the International Youth Hostel Association. They are best avoided.

The Hotel Grande Bretagne, Athens

On Business

*D*espite the artificial boost given by European Union cash injections, Greece's economy remains the most problematic in the EU. Privatisation of a cumbersome public sector was suspended with the election of the PASOK government in 1993, and business is burdened by inefficient bureaucracy. When this book was researched, even EU citizens who wished to work in Greece required a work permit, and getting it involved touring a number of offices, testing for HIV, and a psychiatric evaluation.

Shipping, tourism and agriculture dominate the Greek economy. The shipping industry is in the hands of a relatively small number of private and parastatal companies, but small, family-run operations predominate in farming and tourism.

Many Greek executives are educated in the US, Britain and Canada, and almost all speak fluent English and are familiar with the needs of their overseas colleagues. A new breed of executive sees Europe, rather than the Anglo-Saxon countries, as its role model.

With the collapse of Communism and Soviet influence over its northern Balkan neighbours, Greek business has taken an active interest in the fledgling market-led economies of countries like Bulgaria, Romania, Hungary and even Albania, where the Greek drachma has become the favoured foreign currency. Both Athens and Thessaloníki are well positioned to take advantage of shifts in the Balkan business climate, and the Greek government and business community are keen to forge links with the new economies.

ACCOMMODATION

Major hotel chains including Hilton International, Inter-Continental, Marriott and Novotel have properties in Athens. The capital's two top hotels, the Grande Bretagne and the George V, are both on Syntagma, the city's central square. Greece's major home-grown hotel groups, Astir Hotels, Capsis Hotels and Elektra Hotels, are the best bet for accommodation in regional business capitals such as Thessaloníki and Patras.

BUSINESS ETIQUETTE

Greek business etiquette is relaxed. Punctuality is appreciated, but turning up late for a meeting is not a mortal sin. Normal business wear is jacket and tie for men (a suit is not essential) and skirt or dress for women. Not all Greek offices are air-conditioned, and in summer many executives may dispense with jacket and tie in favour of an open-necked, short-sleeved shirt and slacks. Shake hands on meeting and on parting. Note that many offices close between midday and 4pm.

BUSINESS TRANSPORT
City to city

Olympic Airways operates an extensive inter-city network. Flights should be reserved before you arrive in Greece as they are often overbooked. Air taxi and helicopter charter services are available from Athens and other major airports.

Rapid express trains run between Athens and Thessaloníki (6hr 13min) and Athens and Patras (3hr 26min), but

trains to other points are too slow for the business traveller. Inter-city express buses, which are fast, modern and air-conditioned, offer an alternative.

In the city

Taxis are the most convenient way of getting around big cities but finding one unoccupied can be a problem in Athens. Ask your hotel to book a taxi for vital journeys. Car rental is widely available through international and local companies but few business travellers will want to wrestle with the complexities of Greek one-way systems, city traffic and navigation. Chauffeur-driven cars, the best option if within your budget, can be hired through major hotels and car hire companies.

Communications

The Greek telephone system is antiquated and inefficient and you may have to try repeatedly to get through to the number you want, especially in Athens. Operators are usually helpful and competent in English. Fax facilities are widely available, even in small towns and family-run hotels, and sending a fax message is often easier and less time-consuming than making a phone call. International courier services are also available in Athens, Thessaloníki and Patras.

Conference and exhibition facilities

Greece offers extensive facilities for conferences and exhibitions and is a popular incentive travel destination. Accommodation rates for conference and incentive groups visiting outside peak season are very competitive.

The best conference and exhibition venues are in major international hotels, which are more likely to be able to provide adequate pre-event planning, better communications and more efficient back-up services during the event.

Greece's biggest exhibition centre is in Thessaloníki and offers highly professional event organisation and extensive facilities.
Hellexpo, *Egnatia 154, 546 36 Thessaloníki (tel: 23 92 91 or 29 11 11)*.

Media

Two English-language magazines, *Greece's Weekly* and *Odyssey*, are useful sources of background information for the business traveller. *Balkan News*, launched in 1993, covers business topics in Greece's former socialist bloc neighbours.

Greece's Daily, a news preview distributed by fax, provides news and analysis ahead of the Greek and international daily press.
Balkan News, Greece's Weekly and *Greece's Daily* are published by Balkan Press Ltd, *Alevra 4, 156 69 Papagos, Athens (tel: 6548 208)*.
Odyssey: Zephyr Publications, *Alopekis 20, 106 75 Athens (tel: 725 3995)*.

SECRETARIAL AND TRANSLATION SERVICES

Bilingual secretarial services and translation facilities can be arranged through the business centres of most leading hotels in Athens and Thessaloníki but are not widely available in smaller cities.

Practical Guide

CONTENTS

ARRIVING

By Air

Athens International Airport is the main gateway for charter and scheduled flights to points throughout Europe and worldwide. Thessaloníki International Airport is the northern gateway. Charter airlines fly to Kalámai (Kalamata) and to Préveza between April and October.

Domestic flights are often overbooked. If you plan to fly within Greece, book your flights before you leave home and remember to reconfirm.

Facilities at Greek airports are basic. Car rental companies, taxis, and municipal and private airport shuttle buses offer a choice of transport from Athens International Airport into the city. Elsewhere, the choice is between municipal buses and taxis.

Athens International Airport has two terminals: the western terminal is reserved for Olympic Airways international and domestic flights, and the eastern terminal for all other airlines. A shuttle service operates between them (8.30am–8.30pm). Some airport taxi drivers will overcharge unwary visitors. Insist that the meter is switched on and check that the figure '1' is illuminated, indicating a normal fare. The figure '2', indicating a double fare, should show only between midnight and 6am or for travel outside the city boundaries, which does not apply to the airport.

By Land

The crisis in the former Yugoslavia cut the most convenient overland route to Greece. Road and rail travellers can use ferries from Italy (see below) or travel through Hungary, Romania and Bulgaria.

The *Thomas Cook European Timetable*, published monthly, gives up-to-date details of most rail services and many shipping services throughout Europe and will help you plan a rail journey to, from and around Greece. It is available in the UK from some stations, any branch of Thomas Cook or by phoning 0733

268943. In the USA, contact: **Forsyth Travel Library Inc.**, *9154 West 57th Street (PO BOX 2975), Shawnee Mission, Kansas 66201 (tel: 800 367 7982 toll free).*

By Sea
Frequent ferries connect Igoumenitsa and Patras with the Italian ports of Ancona, Bari, Otranto and Brindisi.

Passports and Visas
Passports are required by all except European Union citizens, who may use national identity cards. British visitors may use a one-year British Visitor's Passport or a full passport. A maximum stay of six months is permitted. Citizens of the USA, Canada, Australia and New Zealand may enter for up to 60 days without a visa. Travellers from South Africa will need a visa. Travellers who require visas should obtain them in their country of residence, as it may prove difficult to obtain them elsewhere. In the UK, the Thomas Cook Passport and Visa Service can advise on and obtain the necessary documentation – consult your Thomas Cook travel consultant.

CAMPING
A list of campsites is available from the Greek National Tourist Office (see **Tourist Offices**, page 189) and from **Association Greek Camping**, *Solonos 102, 10680 Athens (tel: 362 1560).* Camping outside official sites is technically illegal, a rule which is widely ignored.

CHILDREN
There are few special facilities for babies or older children except where provided by package tour companies for their clients. Services provided by holiday companies often include babysitting for younger infants, playgroups for toddlers and activity groups for younger children. Baby milk, food and nappies for infants are available in tourist resorts at most mini-markets and elsewhere from the *geniko emporion* (general store) or from pharmacies.

CLIMATE
Winters are mild and short, with temperatures at their lowest (around 10°C, much colder in the mountains) and rainfall at its highest. By March, days are warmer and April and May offer changeable weather with the possibility of rain balanced by the likelihood of sunshine. Rain rarely falls between June and late September. Midsummer temperatures average more than 30°C. Heatwaves in July and August often bring temperatures of 40°C and above. September temperatures average 25°C and can exceed 30°C.

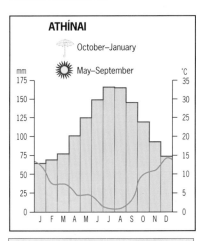

ATHÍNAI

October–January

May–September

WEATHER CONVERSION CHART
25.4mm = 1 inch
°F = 1.8 × °C + 32

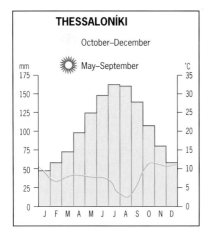

THESSALONÍKI

October–December

May–September

Temperatures drop noticeably through October, but even in December you can often sit outdoors wearing only a light jacket or sweater.

CRIME
Visitors are rarely crime victims. Even Greece's big cities are among the world's safest. That said, normal caution should be exercised. Look after money, travellers' cheques, credit cards and other valuables.

CUSTOMS REGULATIONS
Normal EU rules apply. Non-EU visitors may bring in 200 cigarettes, 50 cigars or 250g of tobacco, one litre of spirits, two litres of wine or liqueurs, 50ml of perfume and 250ml of cologne.
It is forbidden to export antiquities and works of art found in Greece.

DISABLED TRAVELLERS
Facilities for disabled travellers in Greece are poor. Hotel lifts are often too small for wheelchairs and ramps are extremely rare. Pavements – where they exist – are often uneven. Hilly archaeological sites

and steep village streets and steps pose special problems. All arrangements should be checked in advance and needs spelt out. Organisations which may be helpful include **Lavinia Tours**, *Egnatia 101, Thessaloníki 54110*, and the **National Association for Rehabilitation of the Handicapped**, *Hassias, Nea Liossia, KA 1322 Athens.*

DRIVING
Accidents
1 If possible, set up warning signs. In theory, all cars must be equipped with a reflective warning triangle. Not all hire cars are.
2 If someone is injured, the accident must be reported to the police (see page 184). Passers-by in such cases are required to stop and assist. It is advisable to contact the police as a precaution, even if the only damage is material.
3 If you can, write down the names and addresses of other drivers involved, make and licence plates of vehicles, and the names of any witnesses. Write down the date and time of the accident and if possible take photographs from several angles.
4 Under no circumstances admit liability, sign any statement of responsibility, or lose your temper.

Breakdown
The Automobile and Touring Club of Greece (**ELPA**) provides tourist information (tel: 174) and road assistance (tel: 104) 24 hours a day.

Car hire
Rental cars are available from inter-national car hire chains in major cities and resorts and from independent local operators. Renting a car in Greece is expensive and you will find it cheaper to

make arrangements through an international chain such as Holiday Autos, Budget, Eurodollar, Europcar, Hertz or Avis before leaving home. Rental cars are often over-used and under-maintained – check tyres, brakes and steering before leaving the depot. Full collision damage waiver, personal accident, bail bond and liability insurance is essential.

Even major chains often exclude damage to the underside of the vehicle or the tyres from their collision damage waiver provisions. Make sure you have adequate liability insurance to cover such damage.

Documentation
A full British or other EU driving licence is valid for driving in Greece. Most other nationalities require an international driving licence. This can be obtained before you leave home or in Greece from the Automobile and Touring Club of Greece (**ELPA**). You will need your national driving licence, passport and a passport-size photograph. In 1993, **ELPA** charged DR1,500 for this service.

Drink-driving
Blood alcohol content of more than 0.08 per cent is a criminal offence, blood alcohol of between 0.08 and 0.05 per cent a civil offence, and penalties are severe. The best advice is to avoid alcohol altogether when driving.

Fines
Police may impose fines for motoring offences on the spot but may not collect them. The fine must be paid at a Public Treasury office or a bank within 10 days.

Fuel
Petrol costs around the European average. Lead-free fuel is widely available. It is forbidden to carry petrol in a can in the vehicle. Few petrol stations accept credit cards. Petrol stations are not usually self-service.

Navigation, maps and road signs
Romanised spellings of Greek placenames vary. The differences, however, are not so great as to make a name unrecognisable. On main roads, signs are in the Roman alphabet as well as the Greek one. Off the beaten track, signs are often only in Greek, and you will need a working knowledge of the Greek alphabet to find your way (see page 22).

Rules of the road
Speed limits (often ignored) are 50kph in built-up areas, 80kph outside built-up areas and 100kph on motorways. Seatbelts must be worn where fitted. You can be fined for not carrying a warning triangle, fire extinguisher and first-aid kit (many rented cars lack these).

Toll roads
Greece's main toll highway is Odos Ethnikos 1 (National Road 1) between Athens and Thessaloníki, which is overcrowded and under-maintained, with stretches of dual carriageway giving way to stretches of potholed single-track. A second major toll highway connects Athens with Corinth, where it splits, heading south to Tripoli or west to Patras. Tolls are cheap, but unless you are in a hurry the toll roads should be avoided.

ELECTRICITY
Voltage is 220 volts AC. You may require an adaptor for the round two-pin sockets in use in Greece. Power cuts are not uncommon.

EMBASSIES AND CONSULATES

Australia
Mesoghion 15, Athens (tel: 7757 650/4).

Canada
Gennadiou 4, Athens (tel: 7239 510/9).

New Zealand
Semitelou 9, Athens (tel: 7710 112).

United Kingdom
Ploutarchou 1, Athens (tel: 2780 006).

USA
Embassy: *Vasilissis Sofias 91, Athens (tel: 7212 951/9 and 7218 400/1).*
Consulate: *Nikis 59, Thessaloniki (tel: 266121).*

EMERGENCY TELEPHONE NUMBERS

Athens
Medical emergencies: 166
Tourist Police: 171
Fire: 199

Elsewhere in Greece
Ambulance: 166
General Emergency Number: 100
(manned by the police and dealing with crime, fire and medical emergencies)

The Thomas Cook Worldwide Customer Promise offers free emergency assistance at any Thomas Cook Network location to travellers who have purchased their travel tickets at a Thomas Cook location. In addition, any MasterCard cardholder may use any Thomas Cook Network location to report loss or theft of a card and obtain an emergency card replacement as a free service under the Thomas Cook MasterCard International Alliance.

HEALTH

Up-to-date health advice can be obtained from your Thomas Cook travel consultant or direct from the Thomas Cook Travel Clinic, 45 Berkeley Street, London W1A 1EB (tel: 0171 408 4157), which is open for consultation without appointment, 8.30am–5.30pm, Monday to Friday, and can give vaccinations and supply medical advice.

There are no mandatory vaccination requirements and no recommendations other than to keep tetanus and polio vaccination up to date. Vaccination against hepatitis A and typhoid is also recommended if you intend to travel to some of the remoter areas. AIDS is present. Food and water are safe.

All EU countries have reciprocal arrangements for reclaiming the cost of medical services. UK residents should obtain forms CM1 and E111 from any UK post office. Claiming is a laborious and long-drawn-out process and you are only covered for medical care, not for emergency repatriation, holiday cancellation, and so on. You are therefore strongly advised to take out a travel insurance policy to cover all eventualities. You can buy such insurance through the AA, branches of Thomas Cook, and most travel agents.

MEASUREMENTS AND SIZES

Greece uses standard European measurements and sizes (see page 185).

MEDIA

The English-language newspapers *Athens News* (daily) and *Greek News* (weekly) give a quirky insight into national news and views. The bi-monthly glossy magazine *Odyssey* takes a more thoughtful approach. British, US and European newspapers are on sale in Athens and in most holiday resorts the day after publication. English news bulletins are broadcast daily on the ERT2 radio station (98KHz) at 2pm and 9pm. The BBC World Service can be picked up on 9.41, 12.09 and 15.07MHz.

MONEY MATTERS

The Greek currency is the drachma (DR). Coin denominations include 10, 20, 50 and 100 drachma and notes in 100, 500, 1,000 and 5,000 drachmas. Most major currencies, travellers' cheques and Eurocheques can be exchanged at banks, post offices, bureaux de change and travel agencies. The latter two charge a heavier commission but are open when banks and post offices are shut. Banks and post offices are generally open 8am–2pm on weekdays only, but hours may vary.

Credit cards are accepted only in the larger and more expensive hotels, shops and restaurants. MasterCard and Visa are the most widely accepted.

Thomas Cook travellers' cheques free you from the hazards of carrying large amounts of cash and in the event of loss or theft can quickly be refunded. Sterling cheques are recommended, though cheques denominated in US dollars and other major European currencies are accepted. Major hotels, many restaurants and shops, ticket and travel agencies, and car rental offices in main tourist areas accept travellers' cheques in lieu of cash.

The following branches of Thomas Cook can provide emergency assistance in the case of loss or theft of Thomas Cook MasterCard travellers' cheques. They can also provide full foreign exchange facilities and will change currency and cash travellers' cheques (free of commission in the case of Thomas Cook MasterCard travellers' cheques).

Karayeorgias Servias 4, Sindagma, Athens. Thomas Cook Bureau de Change, Othonos Amalias 25, Patras.

Conversion Table

FROM	TO	MULTIPLY BY
Inches	Centimetres	2.54
Feet	Metres	0.3048
Yards	Metres	0.9144
Miles	Kilometres	1.6090
Acres	Hectares	0.4047
Gallons	Litres	4.5460
Ounces	Grams	28.35
Pounds	Grams	453.6
Pounds	Kilograms	0.4536
Tons	Tonnes	1.0160

To convert back, for example from centimetres to inches, divide by the number in the the third column.

Men's Suits

UK	36	38	40	42	44	46	48
Rest of Europe	46	48	50	52	54	56	58
US	36	38	40	42	44	46	48

Dress Sizes

UK	8	10	12	14	16	18
France	36	38	40	42	44	46
Italy	38	40	42	44	46	48
Rest of Europe	34	36	38	40	42	44
US	6	8	10	12	14	16

Men's Shirts

UK	14	14.5	15	15.5	16	16.5	17
Rest of Europe	36	37	38	39/40	41	42	43
US	14	14.5	15	15.5	16	16.5	17

Men's Shoes

UK	7	7.5	8.5	9.5	10.5	11
Rest of Europe	41	42	43	44	45	46
US	8	8.5	9.5	10.5	11.5	12

Women's Shoes

UK	4.5	5	5.5	6	6.5	7
Rest of Europe	38	38	39	39	40	41
US	6	6.5	7	7.5	8	8.5

NATIONAL HOLIDAYS

(see also Festivals, pages 156–7)
Note that Easter and associated moveable feasts are determined by the Greek Orthodox calendar. Dates for Easter can differ from the Western Easter by up to three weeks.
New Year's Day (1 January)
Epiphany
Shrove Monday
Independence Day (25 March)
Good Friday
Easter Sunday
Easter Monday
Labour Day (1 May)
Day of the Holy Spirit
Assumption of the Virgin Mary (15 August)
Ochi Day (28 October)
Christmas Day (25 December)
St Stephen's Day (26 December)

OPENING HOURS

Banks See **Money Matters** page 185.

Museums and Sites

Opening hours given by official sources often bear no relation to those in force at the site or museum, which may change without notice. Most sites officially close at 3pm. Some major sites in Athens stay open longer. Winter hours for these sites are usually shorter than summer (1 April to 31 October) hours.

Shops

Traditionally open from 8am to 1pm and from around 5pm to 8pm, but shops catering to tourists usually stay open longer. Most shops outside tourist areas close on Sunday.

ORGANISED TOURS

Organised tours arranged by travel agencies in Athens can be an affordable way of seeing a number of sights outside the city if you have no transport of your own. Drawbacks include those of travelling with a group. Travel agencies and tour operators at popular resorts also offer a range of tours to sights and beauty spots near by.

PHARMACIES

A green cross marks the *farmakio*. Greek chemists have some medical training and can give advice and prescribe medicines for common ailments. Pharmacies open during normal shop hours and are closed on Saturdays and Sundays.

PLACES OF WORSHIP

Sunday services at most Orthodox churches are held from around 7.30am and last for some hours. Decently dressed (long trousers and shirt sleeves for men, below-the-knee and arm-covering dresses for women) visitors may attend.
Churches of non-Orthodox denominations are found only in Athens, where they include:
Anglican: church of Ayios Pavlos (St Paul) at Filellinon 29
Roman Catholic: church of Ayios Dionysios (St Denis) on Omirou
American inter-denominational: church of Ayios Andreas (St Andrew) on Sina.

POLICE, see Emergency Telephone Numbers.

POSTAL SERVICES

Most larger villages have a post office, distinguished by its prominent circular yellow sign. They are normally open during morning shop hours, but city-centre post offices are also open Saturday mornings. It can often be quicker to change money at a post office than at a bank. Stamps (*grammatosima*) are also sold at kiosks and postcard shops.

Parcels for posting must be inspected by the post office clerk before sealing. Air-mail letters take three to six days to reach the rest of Europe, five to eight days for North America and slightly longer for Australasia. Cards take much longer.

PUBLIC TRANSPORT
Athens Metro
A single line runs from Kifissia in the north through the city centre (Omonia and Monastiraki are the most convenient stops) to Piraeus. Trains run every 15 minutes, from 5am to midnight. Buy your ticket from a machine or ticket booth and validate it as you enter the platform.

Buses
Inter-city buses are cheap, frequent and fast. Athens has two long-haul bus stations. Buses for Évvoia (Evia), Delphi, Ámfissa, Lárisa, Levádhia, Trikkala and the Metéora go from Liossion 260 (*take municipal bus 29 from Amalias, opposite the National Gardens*). Buses for all other destinations go from Kifissou 100 (*take bus 51 from the corner of Vilara and Menandhrou, near Omonia*).
Municipal buses within Athens and Thessaloníki display their number and destination on the front. Tickets can be bought before boarding from ticket booths near main stops or from a *periptero* kiosk. Stamp your ticket in the machine by the door on boarding.

Ferries
Piraeus, the port of Athens, is the main gateway to the Aegean islands. Many nearby islands and points on the Peloponnese coast are served by hydrofoils, some of which go not from the main Piraeus harbour but from Zea Marina, about 3km away. Make sure you know where your boat leaves from. Up-to-date timetables are published monthly by the Greek National Tourist Office (see page 189). Ferries also sail from Rafina (see pages 50–1). Many mainland towns have services to nearby islands. They include:

Alexandroúpolis (*to Thásos, Samothráki*)
Astakós (*to Itháki, Levkás*)
Igoumenítsa (*to Corfu, Paxi*)
Kavala (*to Thásos, Samothráki*)
Killíni (*to Zákinthos, Kefallinía*)
Patras (*to Corfu and other Ionian islands*)
Thessaloníki (*to Thasos, Samothraki, Sporades group*)
Vólos (*to Sporades group*)
Yíthion (*to Kithira, Andikithira, Crete*)

You can change money at banks, bureaux de change, travel agencies and post offices

Taxis

Taxis are cheap and are good value even for long journeys, especially if you are travelling with friends. They should be metered, and most taxi drivers are friendly, honest and helpful (but see **Arriving**, page 180, for possible problems of overcharging). Drivers may pick up other passengers going in the same direction: this will not reduce your fare. In Athens, an empty taxi is often hard to find.

Trains

Trains are cheap but slow, with the exception of the express trains between Athens and Thessaloníki, which take 6 hours 15 minutes. Main routes run between Athens and Thessaloníki (with international connections) on the northern mainland and Athens and Corinth, Patras and Kalamata in the Peloponnese. The most spectacular rail journey in Greece is between Dhiakofton and Kalávrita (see pages 82–3).

SENIOR CITIZENS

Older visitors accustomed to cooler climates may find Greece's fierce midsummer heat unbearable. You may prefer to travel before mid-June or after mid-September, when the weather will be warm but not punishing. Just as Greeks love children, they also respect older people. On the other hand, they also expect them to fend for themselves – for example, when boarding a bus – and in a country where queueing is unknown this can be trying.

TELEPHONES

The easiest way to call is from a metered phone in a street kiosk. You pay at the end of the call. Many shops and small hotels also have metered phones, as do campsites and travel and ticket agencies in resorts. Few of them allow calls using AT&T or similar charge cards. Metered phones are also available in booths at offices of OTE (Greek Telecommunications Organisation). These are cheaper, but hours are less convenient.

Dialling codes from Greece are:
Australia: 0061
Canada and the USA: 001
New Zealand: 0064
UK and Ireland: 0044
International operator: 161

In this book, local area codes are included in all telephone numbers except in the Athens and Thessaloníki sections. Dialling codes within Greece for the three major cities are:
Athens: 01
Patras: 061
Thessaloníki: 031

TIME

GMT + 2 (+ 3 in summer). Clocks change in spring and autumn on the same date as other EU countries, but the time change does not always coincide with other countries such as the USA.

TIPPING

Service is included in restaurants but it is normal to leave small change on the table as an additional tip. This is also usual in bars and cafés. There is no pressure to tip in hotels but a small tip will be welcomed. Inflation makes it impossible to be more specific; in 1993 a tip of DR100 was acceptable, a tip of 500 excessive. In taxis, 'keep the change' is normal practice.

TOILETS

Standards vary enormously but have improved dramatically in recent years.

Toilets in cafés and tavernas are usually better than public facilities. Greek plumbing is narrow-bore and easily blocked, and in most place you are requested not to flush toilet paper but to put it in the waste bin provided. Only the latest modern hotels are exceptions.

TOURIST INFORMATION
The Greek National Tourist Office (GNTO) has offices worldwide and provides a range of information which includes hotel listings for all parts of the country, up-to-date transport schedules, and information on archaeological sites, exhibitions, festivals, and other events.

Abroad:
Australia
51–7 Pitt Street, Sydney NSW 200 (tel: 02 241 1663)
Canada
1300 Bay Street, Main Level, Toronto, Ontario M5R 3K8 (tel: 416 968 2220)
1223 Rue de la Montagne, Montreal, Quebec H3G 1Z2 (tel: 514 871 1535)
United Kingdom
4 Conduit Street, London W1R ODJ (tel: 071 734 5997)
USA
645 Fifth Avenue, New York NY 10022 (tel: 212 421 5777)

168 North Michigan Avenue, Chicago IL 60601 (tel: 312 728 1084)
611 West 6th Street, Suite 1998, Los Angeles CA 90017 (tel: 213 626 6696)

In Greece:
Athens
Karayeorgi Servias 2 (tel: 01 322 2545) (in the National Bank building on Platia Syntagma)
Delfi (Delphi)
Vass. Pavlou-Friderikis 44 (tel: 0265 82900)
Ioánnina
Nap. Zerva 2 (tel: 0651 25086)
Kaválla
Filellinon 5 (tel: 051 228762/231653)
Platia Elevtherias (tel: 051 222425)
Navplion
Platia Iatrou (tel: 0752 24444)
Olympia
Praxitelous Kondili (tel: 0624 23100)
Patras
Iroon Politekhniou, Glifadha (tel: 061 420303)
Thessaloníki
Mitropoleos 34 (tel: 031 222935)
Vólos
Platia Riga Fereou (tel: 0421 23500)

The Athens Metro system is elderly but is also a quick and cheap way of getting around

ACKNOWLEDGEMENTS

The Automobile Association wishes to thank the following organisations, libraries and photographers for their assistance in the preparation of this book.

MARY EVANS PICTURE LIBRARY 15, 60b, 62/3, 63a, 90/1, 95; **ROBERT GAULDIE** 64b, 113, 139a; **HILTON INTERNATIONAL** 175; **TERRY HARRIS** 5, 24, 25, 135, 142, 146, 149, 159b; **THE MANSELL COLLECTION LTD** 14a, 14b, 59, 132a, 132b; **NATURE PHOTOGRAPHERS LTD** 136 (P R Sterry), 137b (E A Janes), 138 (K Blamire), 139b (A Cleave); **SPECTRUM COLOUR LIBRARY** 119.

The remaining photographs are held in the AA Photo Library and were taken by Terry Harris with the exception of the cover and pages 19, 33, 34b, 37b, 38, 39b, 40, 43, 47, 48, 52, 56, 58, 60a, 61, 62/3, 65, 66, 67, 69, 72, 75a, 75b, 88, 104, 105, 123, 125, 140, 174, 177, taken by Richard Surman, and pages 150b, 151b, 151c, 157, 160, 161a, 179, taken by Peter Wilson, and the spine taken by Tim Larsen-Collinge.

The author thanks the following companies for their help in providing transport to and accommodation in Greece: British Airways; Holiday Autos; Intercontinental Hotels; and Virgin Atlantic Airways.

CONTRIBUTORS

Series adviser: Melissa Shales **Designer:** Design 23 **Copy editor:** Ron Hawkins
Verifier: Joanna Whitaker **Indexer:** Marie Lorimer